"This superb book will help save lives."

—*General Barry McCaffrey*
Former director, Office of National Drug Control Policy

"An important new book. A godsend for older adults and those who care for them. Here readers will find easy-to-understand explanations for the specific problems of addiction and clear paths to lifelong recovery."

—*Robert L. DuPont, M.D.*
Former director, National Institute on Drug Abuse (NIDA)
Former director, Office of National Drug Control Policy
Author, The Selfish Brain: Learning from Addiction

"*Aging and Addiction* offers practical approaches for older people, family members, and those working with the elderly, while promoting the dignity, well-being, self-determination, and contributions of older adults."

—*James Firman*
President and CEO, The National Council on the Aging

"*Aging and Addiction* offers research and clinical literature on late-life alcohol and medication problems that are a growing public health threat. For health care and treatment professionals, older adults, and family members."

—*Frederic C. Blow, Ph.D.*
Senior associate research scientist, department of psychiatry,
University of Michigan
Cochair, Huss Research on Older Adults and Alcohol/Drug Problems

"Finally, a book that supports families helping older adults maintain independence, sobriety, and joy of life."

—*Max Schneider, M.D., F.A.S.A.M.*
Clinical professor of psychiatry (addiction medicine),
University of California/Irvine
Former president of the American Society of Addiction Medicine (ASAM)
Former chair of the board of directors, National Council on
Alcoholism and Drug Dependence (NCADD)

"Clearly written, filled with well-told stories, helpful resources, this book will help young and old alike grasp the facts about the unique problems associated with older adults' addiction."

—*Katherine Ketcham*
Coauthor of Under the Influence, The Spirituality of Imperfection, *and* Beyond the Influence

"Finally, a book that debunks the misperceptions of aging and addiction! The authors expose an endemic social issue far too long confined to the dark and most importantly show the way back to a better life."

—*Jim McDonough*
Director, Florida Office of Drug Control
Former director of strategy, Office of National Drug Control Policy

"Colleran and Jay clarify that age is no barrier to addiction. And neither should it be an obstacle to recovery."

—*William C. Moyers*
Former president, Johnson Institute

"A great book! A well-written guide . . . to help families understand the relationship between aging and addiction and recognize the treatment needs of older adults."

—*Robert G. La Prad*
Director, Bishop's Council on Alcohol and Other Drugs
Board of directors, National Catholic Council on Alcohol

"A compelling, intelligent, readable book. A singular masterpiece of compassion."

—*Paul McGann, M.D., F.R.C.P.C.*
Clinical director, J. Paul Sticht Center on Aging and Rehabilitation,
Wake Forest Baptist Medical Center

"An authoritative reference for anyone who wonders if substance abuse lurks behind an older adult's cognitive decline or unexplained progression of medical and mental health issues."

—Lance Mynderse, M.D.
Son of recovering older adult parents

"*Aging and Addiction* helped me help my dad find treatment, sobriety, and ultimately serenity."

—Eric M., son of a recovering parent

AGING &
ADDICTION

Helping Older Adults Overcome
Alcohol or Medication Dependence

*Carol Colleran &
Debra Jay*

with a foreword by
General Barry McCaffrey

HAZELDEN®

Hazelden
Center City, Minnesota 55012-0176

1-800-328-0094
1-651-213-4590 (Fax)
www.hazelden.org

ISBN: 1-56838-792-X

14 13 12   6 5

Cover design by David Spohn
Interior design by Ann Sudmeier
Typesetting by Stanton Publication Services, Inc.

*Dedicated to the memory of
my beautiful, funny,
quirky, wonderful grandmother:
Marcella Ann Carlson.*

—**Debra Jay**

*To my children:
Cathy, my guardian angel, who showed me
a new purpose for life after fifty;
Dan, who made it all possible by making me his yearlong project;
Amy, who gives me ongoing encouragement and nurturing;
Jay, who helped me find the courage to move forward.*

—**Carol Colleran**

Contents

Foreword

by General Barry McCaffrey

This superb book will help save lives. It's that simple. *Aging and Addiction* is intelligent, readable, and well researched. Above all, it is an immensely compassionate book, which offers hope and direction to families and readers who have an older adult who is abusing alcohol or medications.

Older American adults who abuse or are addicted to alcohol or prescription medications are not failures. Most have raised wonderful families, retired from successful careers and community activities, and led energetic lives. They are suffering from a disease. As with any other physical illness, they can be helped to recover. However, many go without diagnosis or even minimal treatment from their doctors and the health care community.

Substance abuse among older adults is often ignored or even denied by family members and health care workers. The health care industry has not adequately provided solutions for older people dealing with addiction. None of us wants to believe that these dear older adults who cared for or mentored us in our youth are now abusing prescription medications or alcohol. If abuse or addiction is suspected, many family members deny the problem by protesting, "They have only a few years left. Let them enjoy themselves. They aren't hurting anyone." Colleran and Jay make clear that these older adults aren't enjoying their "few years left." Instead, they are causing themselves and those who love them acute misery. Addiction keeps older adults from "reevaluating life to create deeper meaning, experiencing the freedom of and comfort with who [they] are, achieving personal integrity, developing a more encompassing view of life itself, giving back to the community, and celebrating place among family and friends."

Those who are best positioned to help these beloved older

people often turn away from the problem in dismay. Their failure to intervene is not cruelty, but ignorance and denial. *Aging and Addiction* rallies everyone—family members, medical professionals, spiritual leaders, and those involved in the elderly care industry—to come to the aid of these men and women who spent their earlier decades loving and caring for us. First, we need to learn about older adult addiction and how to effectively intervene. *Aging and Addiction* is a good place to begin our education. It offers reliable research, vital medical information, compelling testimonies, and guidance from authors with expertise in their fields. Carol Colleran, director and pioneer of older adult treatment at Hanley-Hazelden in West Palm Beach, Florida, and Debra Jay, interventionist and coauthor of *Love First: A New Approach to Intervention for Alcoholism and Drug Addiction,* encourage family members, health care professionals, and the managed care industry to openly and diligently redress the social problem of substance abuse by older adults. We need to face up to these questions before the giant baby-boomer generation becomes senior citizens. The bottom line is that older adults deserve every opportunity to live their lives in the best of health and happiness.

As past director of the White House Office of National Drug Control Policy, I am sadly aware of the toll that addiction takes on older adults. The disease of addiction excludes no one. Colleran and Jay write that "Aging parents, grandparents, and friends have a valuable and irreplaceable role to play in our lives, the lives of our children, and in our communities. When addiction claims them, everybody loses." A few statistics might help illustrate how alcohol and medication dependence affects society.

According to the Center on Alcohol and Substance Abuse at Columbia University, in 1998 health care costs of substance abuse in older adults reached $30 billion. This cost is expected to rise to an estimated $100 billion by the year 2018. America is now burdened with over three million older adults in the United States who suffer from alcohol or medication dependency. Older adults who are not treated stand a very poor chance of living alone into old age. Most will need some type of assisted living, which will not only be costly for families but every health insurance holder. When older adults are treated early, however, most will remain self-sufficient much longer, enjoying their lives, families, and communities.

Currently, 98 percent of the $10 billion spent on hospital admissions for older adults with alcohol and medication addiction is expenditures for the consequences of that disease, such as hip fractures, liver and kidney disease, depression, gastrointestinal problems, dementia, and a host of other health problems. Less than 2 percent is actually spent on treating the primary illness of addiction. Many of the symptoms of addiction mimic other illnesses and are sometimes overlooked, making it less likely that an older adult will receive proper treatment.

Alcohol and medication dependence is one of the most severe health care challenges facing older adults. In September 1998 the American Medical Association reported that more older adults are admitted to hospitals for alcohol- and drug-related illnesses or injuries than for heart problems. However, the medical profession has been poorly trained and supervised on prescribing medication for older adults. Data from the Veterans Affairs hospital system suggest that "Elderly patients may be prescribed inappropriately high doses of medications such as benzodiazepines and may be prescribed these medications for longer periods than are younger adults. In general, older people should be prescribed lower doses of medications, because the body's ability to metabolize many medications decreases with age."

In addition, an article in the National Institute on Drug Abuse Research Report Series entitled "Prescription Drugs: Abuse and Addiction" states that "The misuse of prescription drugs may be the most common form of drug abuse among the elderly. Elderly persons use prescription medications approximately three times as frequently as the general population and have been found to have the poorest rates of compliance with directions for taking a medication."

We need to demand that public health policy in America address the medical issue of substance abuse by older adults. It will continue to cost America a fortune in lost resources and lives if we do *not* provide education and treatment for older adults and their families.

The primary goal of the White House Office of National Drug Control Policy is "to help people stop using drugs and maintain drug-free lifestyles while achieving productive functioning within families, at work, and in society. Providing access to treatment . . . is a worthwhile endeavor. It is both compassionate public policy and a sound investment." This superb book, *Aging and Addiction,* is a valuable tool for an entire generation. In my view, this excellent work will help families directly address the problems of substance abuse with responsible, loving action. We must support the needs of our older loved ones without bullying or shaming. The end result will be older Americans who will rediscover wholesome and robust living.

Aging and Addiction is a superb tutorial to help senior Americans with alcohol and medication dependence. This book will serve as a benchmark for any future publications on this painful issue. Carol Colleran and Debra Jay provide exhaustive research and share their enormous experience to help families identify health problems related to addiction. Those of us who are sandwiched between two generations, caring for our children as well as the elderly, will welcome this book, which provides a sensible approach to dealing with aging parents, relatives, or friends. This book is intended primarily to help families and friends of older adults through the confusion, sorrow, and darkness of addiction. However, physicians, clergy, psychiatrists, pharmacists, social workers, and caregivers can also benefit immensely from this powerful piece of work.

Aging and Addiction will not only help saves lives, but will enrich them as well.

General Barry McCaffrey
December 2001

Acknowledgments

We have deep gratitude for the many older adults and families we have worked with through the years. We have learned so much from them. We also thank the two women who allowed us to print the intervention letters they wrote to the addicted older adults they love.

Thank you to our editor, Richard Solly, for his confidence, encouragement, assistance, and patience. His faith in us gave us faith in ourselves. We greatly appreciate and thank General Barry McCaffrey for kindly agreeing to write the foreword.

We greatly appreciate the help of Max A. Schneider, M.D., and Robert L. DuPont, M.D., who generously provided information from their publications and offered suggestions and comments. Heartfelt thanks to Robert M. Morse, M.D., and Lance Mynderse, M.D., for reviewing the manuscript and sharing their invaluable thoughts, and to Sr. Patrice Selby, I.H.M., Med., C.A.P., M.A.C., who shared her expertise on older adults and grief.

We also thank the following people for their much-needed contributions: Fred Blow, Ph.D., Jerry Boriskin, Ph.D., Bill Lamp, Giff Dean, Jerry Singleton, Walter Trenschel, Ph.D., Steve Millette, Kathleen Kissane, Tom Early, Adele Kemp, Jayne Johnson, Michael Counes, Jim Dopp, Dan Zondervan, and Terry Lehman. We thank Nancy Solak for her excellent proofreading.

Thanks to all of our friends and relatives for their support. Thanks to Beth Loew for suggestions, Lori Forseth Koneczny for listening, and Arnie Eisele and Al Eisele for helping. A big thanks to Jeff Jay, who took the time to read drafts and give astute suggestions, for being the ballast while this book was being written.

A special thanks to Marion Danens, whose example teaches that, like a garden well tended, life produces beauty and excellence when helping others is the seed we sow and nurture.

Finally, deep appreciation to Maurice Forseth, who showed us how to age with vitality, purpose, and generosity of spirit.

Be a Lamp, a lifeboat, a ladder.
Help someone's soul heal.
Walk out of your house like a shepherd.

—Rumi

Family Responses to Addicted Older Adults

Addiction Isn't One of Life's Last Pleasures

"I'm not going to take away one of Dad's last pleasures in life." When speaking of an aging parent's use of alcohol and medications, many people commonly mistake addiction for pleasure. Confusing the pleasure of having a glass of wine at dinner with the devastation of addiction is most prevalent when we talk about people in the retirement years. This misconception also reflects our attitudes about the value of life in later years, implying: "There really isn't much for him to enjoy anymore, so why shouldn't he spend his time drinking? Who does it hurt?" "He's worked hard his whole life. He deserves to reward himself now." Addiction isn't a reward, and it isn't one of life's last pleasures. Addiction is a thief. It robs older people of the most important years in their lives.

These late years bear a great gift, a special readiness to grow in ways not possibly imagined before. In the words of former president Jimmy Carter: "The virtues of aging include both the blessings that come to us as we grow older and what we have to offer that might be beneficial to others." This is the age to integrate life experience, knowledge, and spirituality. The later years are for reevaluating life to create deeper meaning, experiencing the freedom of and comfort with who you are, achieving personal integrity, developing a more encompassing view on life itself, giving back to the community, and celebrating family and friends. The addicted older adult is blocked from these growth experiences. Alcohol and other drug addictions close the door to this phase of life.

Once, a seventy-year-old widow named Audrey came to us after her doctor recommended treatment for her addiction to alcohol and mood-altering prescription drugs. Her health was failing fast, she was unable to care for herself, and she suffered from deep depression. Her doctor correctly diagnosed her primary problem as addiction.

When Audrey came to the treatment center, she was in a wheelchair. Her unsteady gait caused her to walk with fear of stumbling or falling. She was covered with large black bruises and burns from her kitchen stove. She no longer had an appetite, so she ate little and was emaciated. Her skin had lost its elasticity and seemed to hang from her bones. Her eyes had the watery, aged look of a ninety-year-old. One night, she passed out in her driveway and scraped her face. The next morning, her neighbor found her face down on the pavement in her nightgown.

Audrey couldn't be trusted with the grandchildren anymore, so family visits were fewer and farther between. Her son checked up on her, but often Audrey didn't remember he had visited. She rarely showered and spent most days sitting in a chair alternating between drinking, sleeping, and watching television. She stopped calling friends, and social invitations had long since ceased.

She never cleaned house anymore. Old newspapers, unopened mail, and dirty dishes littered the living room. Her children would come by to straighten things up and do the laundry when they could, but the demands of their spouses, children, and jobs made that difficult.

Audrey went to several different doctors for prescriptions for Valium, a tranquilizer, and Placidyl, a sleep inducer. Both medications, addictive and having more adverse side effects on patients over sixty, should only be used for short periods of time. Mixed with alcohol, they can cause heavy sedation, even death. Audrey had taken both medications for years at three to four times the prescribed dosage. She mixed them with large quantities of alcohol. She was a full-fledged addict, though her drugs were legal—alcohol and prescription medications.

By the time Audrey arrived for treatment, she was at the end stage of her addiction—a place close to death. Her children knew she had a problem, but they didn't know what to do. They were paralyzed with indecision for two main reasons: They lacked good information about addiction, and they couldn't agree among themselves on the best way to help her. Over time, they became desensitized to the seriousness of her problem and began to explain the addiction as "just the way Mom is." So the problem progressed to a dangerously advanced stage. Luckily for Audrey, she was referred to a new doctor who recognized her addiction and understood that successful recovery usually begins with professional alcohol and drug treatment.

Once Audrey was in treatment and weaned off the alcohol, Valium, and Placidyl, she bloomed. She was in a program designed for people her own age. She attended lectures, group therapy, and grief group. Her children came to the family program. Audrey's memory improved, her appetite returned, she regained her energy, and she started walking, swimming, and exercising every day. She made friends in treatment and learned the importance of working a recovery program once she returned home.

Ten years later, Audrey is still sober. She plays an important role in her grandchildren's lives, went on a trip to Ireland with her daughter, goes on cruises with friends, gardens, and dates a gentleman she met at church. Recovery from addiction brought pleasure back into her life. She lives creatively and with meaning.

May Sarton, poet, novelist, and avid gardener, says of old age in her book *At Seventy: A Journal:*

> I had been asked to talk about old age . . . [and] said, "This is the best time of my life. I love being old." At that point a voice from the audience asked loudly, "Why is it good to be old?" I answered spontaneously and a little on the defensive, for I sensed incredulity in the questioner, "Because I am more myself than I have ever been. There is less conflict, I am happy, more balanced, and (I heard myself say rather aggressively) *more powerful.*"

If you are concerned about an older person with an addiction, don't let his age lull you into thinking his life is over and what he does doesn't really matter. Learn about the disease of addiction, treatment, and recovery. Aging parents, grandparents, and friends have a valuable and irreplaceable role to play in our lives, the lives of our children, and in our communities. When addiction claims them, everybody loses.

⚏

A Few Things You Should Know

Addiction is the same disease regardless of which drug is used: alcohol, mood-altering medications, or illicit drugs. Drugs have different effects—some stimulate us, others calm us down. Some drugs have a faster addictive cycle than others. We place more stigma on illegal drugs than legal drugs. We call addiction by different names: *alcoholism, drug addiction,* or *chemical dependency.* Each term describes the same disease. We will use these terms interchangeably throughout the book. If we use the word *alcoholic,* we are referring to all addicted people regardless of the type of drug they use. If we use the word *addict,* we are referring to people who are addicted to alcohol as well as people who are addicted to other drugs.

We employ different terms to describe people suffering from this disease: *alcoholic, addict, substance abuser.* Each term describes the addicted. However, *substance abuser* describes people who are suffering from the disease of addiction and people who may not yet be addicted, but are *misusing* substances. Older adults, for the most part, do not use illicit drugs. A very small percentage of this population is addicted to marijuana, cocaine, crack, or heroin. This is expected to change as baby boomers age.

Addiction to alcohol or other drugs, including prescription

drugs, is an equal opportunity disease. It affects men and women, young and old, rich and poor, the uneducated and the highly educated, and people of every color. No one who chooses to use a mood-altering substance can predict with certainty whether they will become addicted. Since addiction affects both men and women, we have alternated the use of the pronouns *he* and *she* throughout the book.

Older adult is a designation replacing *senior citizen* when we refer to people over the age of fifty-five. *Senior citizen* is often associated with negative stereotypes and age-related prejudices, while *older adult* is increasingly accepted as a more respectful way to acknowledge people in the later stages of life.

Ⅲ

Wrong Thinking Blocks Right Action

Audrey's children loved her dearly. There was no question about that. Although they were frustrated and sometimes angry, that was a normal response to the tough situation they'd been dealing with for years. Their inability to help their mother wasn't for lack of love or concern; it was for lack of good information. The many myths and misconceptions about addiction misled them. Everyone had a different idea of what was right, no one could agree on what to do, and there was much bickering and indecision, which added to their frustration and anger. The lack of good information caused wrong thinking, and wrong thinking blocked their ability to take the right action.

Anyone facing an older relative's alcohol or medication dependence must begin by separating fact from fiction. Identify the myths and replace them with truth. When everybody is on the same page and works from the same information, it is easier to make well-informed, cohesive family decisions.

Let's take a look at the most common myths and misconceptions about addiction in older adults:

- *It's temporary. She's drinking to overcome her grief (loneliness, insomnia, and so on).* People drink for many different reasons: to follow social customs, reduce stress, unwind at the end of the day, lower inhibitions, alleviate boredom, self-medicate grief—the list goes on. Choosing alcohol to solve problems is always an unhealthy choice. Alcohol only masks problems and prevents people from working through their issues. If the drinking stops, the problems still exist.

  Sometimes the drinking doesn't stop. Instead, it triggers the disease of chemical dependency. When this happens, the older person now drinks only to satisfy her addiction. Even if all her problems were solved, she'd still drink. The disease is in charge, and it has taken away her ability to consistently control her alcohol use.

- *He's always been strong willed. He says he can get his drinking under control on his own.* Addiction is a disease that cripples the will; it is a brain disease. In other words, addiction isn't controlled by willpower; willpower is disabled by addiction. Family members are often confused by the nature of addiction. Loss of control doesn't happen all at once. It occurs slowly over time and tends to be periodic. The addicted person seems to have control one day but not the next. It helps to understand that once the first drink or pill is taken, the addicted person cannot predict whether or not he'll lose control. But, with continued alcohol and drug use, we can be certain that loss of control will happen. We just don't know when.

  As the disease worsens, loss of control occurs more frequently and for longer periods. When an addicted person is in the late stages of the disease, the loss of control is almost complete.

- *She can't be addicted. Her doctor prescribes the pills she takes.* Many medications are mood-altering, addictive drugs. While they may play an important role in medicine, a certain number of people who use them can become addicted. Doctors prescribing drugs to older patients can be influenced by *ageism*—prejudices and stereotypes that shape our thinking about what it means to be old. A doctor's beliefs about aging may lead to unnecessary or excessive drug therapies for older patients. Medications are often substituted for other needed therapies, such as counseling, biofeedback, relaxation techniques, behavior modification, local electrical stimulation, exercise, diet, or other drug-free ways to solve problems.

Consider the statistics. Older women consume 60 percent of all prescription and over-the-counter medications. The number of prescriptions written for older adults averages fifteen prescriptions per older person per year. Eighty-three percent of people over sixty-five use prescription medications, and approximately 16.9 million of these prescriptions are for tranquilizers. Although it's true that older adults have increased medical needs, these statistics beg the question: *Are our elders overmedicated?*

Many things can lead to medication addiction. For example, a sleep inducer that shouldn't be used for more than a week or two is instead prescribed for several years for an older patient's complaints of insomnia. An older person may mix addictive medications with alcohol, hastening the progression of addiction. The pleasurable effects of tranquilizers may cause her to use them more than recommended. If she suffers from undiagnosed alcoholism and mixes in a synthetic opiate pain medication, the existing addiction advances to a dangerous stage.

Once addiction takes hold, more of the drug is required

to achieve the same effect. As a result, older adults often go to several doctors to seek additional prescriptions. Ageism prevents many doctors from viewing good-natured grandmothers as drug addicts, and, therefore, they are less observant of their drug-seeking behaviors. We've seen older people who can barely function at home clean up quite nicely to make a good appearance in the doctor's office when they're requesting prescriptions for tranquilizers, sleep inducers, or pain pills.

- *It's unlikely someone my grandfather's age will become alcoholic or addicted to other drugs.* The fastest-growing population of alcoholics is seventy-five-year-old widowers. Addiction does not discriminate based on age. Whether the drug of choice is alcohol, mood-altering medications, or illegal drugs, no one becomes immune from addiction by growing older. If anything, the physical changes that occur with age, especially the slowing of the ability to metabolize substances out of the body, allow alcohol and other drugs to stay in the body longer and have a greater impact on the brain and other organs. Health problems and the use of multiple medications further increase the toll.

- *My grandfather's too old to change.* Older adults not only can change, but they have the highest rate of success in treatment of any age group. Treatment may take longer because of complex detoxification and more elaborate medical issues, but the ability to follow through with commitments and strong work ethics serves our elders well in building lasting programs of recovery.

- *My mother suffers from heart disease. Research shows that drinking alcohol is good for her heart.* Popular media has been responsible for spreading the "good news" about alcohol consumption, but has left out the details of the many risks. The media rarely mentions that you shouldn't drink if you take medications, have health problems, or have a family history of alcoholism. It doesn't mention that benefits are found only in a small percentage of people and are dwarfed by enormous risks. Alcohol is linked to strokes, cancer, irregular heartbeats, high blood pressure, addiction, and sudden death. If you're older, you're at higher risk for the negative consequences of alcohol use.

Dr. Ira Goldberg, speaking for the American Heart Association, says:

> We want to make clear that there are other risk-reduction options that are well-documented and free of the potential hazards associated with alcohol consumption. Our advice: If you want to reduce your risk of heart disease, talk to your doctor about lowering your cholesterol and blood pressure, controlling your weight, getting enough exercise, and following a healthy diet. There is no scientific proof that drinking wine or any other alcoholic beverage can replace these effective conventional measures.

Alcohol is responsible for a significant percentage of the illnesses and deaths in the United States every year. A report released in 2001 by the Robert Wood Johnson Foundation concludes that substance abuse and addiction continues to be the leading health problem in the United States.

The U.S. House of Representatives Select Committee on Aging found that 70 percent of hospitalized people over the age of sixty were admitted for illnesses and accidents related to alcohol. Alcohol-related hospital care for older patients costs $60 billion a year. Fifty percent of nursing home residents have problems caused by alcohol.

• *You can't help someone until he wants help. Treatment won't work if we force him to go.* This is possibly the most damaging myth of all. It allows the disease of chemical dependency to progress unchecked. People who are chemically dependent don't spontaneously decide to get help for their addiction. Something happens in their life that causes them to want help.

An older person left to find help in her own time is at high risk of dying first. Addiction causes illnesses that resemble problems associated with old age. Doctors may treat these illnesses without diagnosing the underlying problem of alcoholism. As long as the alcoholism goes untreated, the illnesses will persist, and the elder patient's health will continue to decline.

Ask yourself this question: "If an alcoholic won't get help until she wants help, what will make her want help?" A recent poll of recovering people found that 70 percent sought help only after family, friends, or co-workers intervened. Another study, conducted over twenty-five years, found that success in treatment was the same for people ordered into treatment by the courts and people who chose to go in on their own. It is not how someone gets into treatment that counts, but what happens once they're there.

William Bennett, drug czar under former president George Bush, wrote in an editorial in the *Washington Post:* "One clear fact about drug treatment is that success in treatment is a function of time in treatment. And time in treatment is often a function of coercion—being forced into treatment by a loved one, an employer or, as is often the case, the legal system." Families that worry about *forcing* an older loved one often overlook the option of effectively *asking* them to enter treatment by implementing a loving, structured family intervention.

- *At her age, what difference does it make?* This is a version of the myth we talked about in the first chapter. This thinking is influenced by ageism and the stereotype that older people have little value. Many of the greatest psychologists and religious teachers would say that the later years are the most important years for spiritual growth, self-actualizing, and modeling personal integrity for younger generations. Robert C. Atchley writes in *Continuity and Adaptation in Aging:* "Psychological development in later adulthood is much more obvious in integrative functions such as wisdom and transcendence." Describing the later part of his life, Kirk Douglas, in his book *Climbing the Mountain: My Search for Meaning,* concurs. He writes that his greatest personal and spiritual growth came only after he was seventy years old.

Challenge the myths you've accepted as fact and ask your family members to do the same. Together, you can make a huge difference and may even save your aging relative's life.

⚊

Alcoholism Accelerates Aging

Mary Pipher, author of *Another Country: Navigating the Emotional Terrain of Our Elders,* explains the difference between *young-old* and *old-old:* "Loss of health is what delineates the two stages of old age. Until people lose their health, they are in the young-old category. Until people are ill, many keep their old routines and add some new pleasurable ones. Even if they lose their spouses, they still can enjoy friends and family. Retired people travel, do volunteer work, pursue creative activities, and play cards or golf. However, poor health changes everything."

Addiction makes the old, older. A young-old person remains active, healthy, and independent long into retirement. The old-old person begins the downward journey into illness, dependence, pain, and inactivity. Chemical dependency can take the young-old and transform them into the old-old before their time.

Older men and women are increasingly *frangible*—readily or easily damaged, even if they don't appear delicate or frail. This vulnerability does not stand up well to addiction. When addiction takes hold, the young-old begin to develop the problems of the old-old: memory loss, shaky hands, frequent napping, confusion, incontinence, boredom, depression, falls, bruises, and dizziness. We've seen fifty-eight-year-old men look and act like unhealthy eighty-five-year-olds.

What does this mean for those of us close to the addicted older adult? Everything about our relationships begins to change. Grown children, in the middle of raising their own families, are unexpectedly faced with a profusion of complicated and time-consuming problems. The spouse, still in the young-old stage, is grieving the loss of a vital life partner to addiction. Grandchildren are cheated out of the wonderful experiences that come only from close relationships with grandparents. Mary Pipher explains the importance of connections with grandparents: "A teacher told me that she can tell which kids in her class have relationships with grandparents or other older people. They are quieter, calmer, and more trusting." Pipher goes on to say: "Grandparents grew up in a slower world. . . . [They] have plenty of time for children—time to sit on a porch and watch a bird build a nest or a squirrel gather acorns; time to read stories or help with a stamp collection or a ham radio."

In terms of transporting our elders into the world of the old-old, alcohol is the most harmful of all drugs. It's the drug of choice for older adults and the most damaging drug to the human body. It impacts virtually every organ system. Let's take a close look. The following is adapted from a report published by Case Western Reserve University's School of Medicine:

> *Heart:* With aging, the cardiovascular system undergoes many changes that predispose older persons to heart conditions, especially heart failure, coronary artery disease, and defects in the

heart's conduction system. Alcohol increases the amount of cholesterol and fatty acids in the body. It increases the workload of the heart, causes arrhythmia or an abnormal heart rhythm, and causes inflammation of the heart muscle called myocarditis, a condition that can lead to heart failure. Alcohol can cause high blood pressure or hypertension. A new study found that consuming more than two beers or ten ounces of wine per day was a greater risk factor for coronary artery disease than smoking.

Brain: Long after age slows the body, the brain continues to function normally. For most, age doesn't affect cognition. But alcohol does. It impairs judgment, reasoning, learning, coordination, memory, and speech. It acts upon the central nervous system, which controls behavior, and has a sedative effect that can result in death. Prolonged, heavy drinking can cause brain damage.

Pancreas: Alcohol irritates pancreatic cells and blocks the digestive juices from passing into the small intestine. It causes pancreatitis, a condition where digestive juices build up and begin to digest the pancreas. This is extremely painful and can result in death. Alcohol can be a source of secondary diabetes by interfering with insulin production.

Bones and blood: Alcohol contributes to osteoporosis, which causes brittle and easily broken bones. Alcohol leads to a loss of calcium, lowers one's ability to fight off disease, causes anemia, and increases the likelihood of bruising. Alcohol reduces red and white blood cell production. Red blood cells are needed to carry oxygen from the lungs to the body tissues, and white blood cells to fight infections and inflammation.

Digestive traçt: Alcohol affects the health of the esophagus, stomach, and intestines. It irritates the lining of the digestive tract; causes gastritis, bleeding, ulcers, perforations in the wall of the tract; swelling that causes obstructions of passageways; and colitis. Aging bodies are less able to absorb nutrients, and alcohol further reduces absorption of vitamin B and minerals such as zinc, calcium, and magnesium. *Lack of vitamin B* causes a wide range of symptoms including eczema of the face, sleeplessness, thinning of the hair, depression, stomach irritation, memory loss, disorientation, instability, hearing loss, headaches, visual disturbances, staggering, congestive heart failure, loss of sensation in the legs and feet, paralysis, and more. *Lack of zinc* leads to poor night vision, decreased sense of taste and smell, reduced ability to ward off infections, and poor healing of wounds. *Lack of calcium* negatively affects the health of bones and teeth, the heartbeat, blood coagulation, transmission of nerve impulses, muscle contraction and relaxation, stimulation of hormones, and activation of enzymes. *Lack of magnesium* leads to irritability, irregular heartbeat, and weakening of muscles.

Kidneys: Alcohol causes inflammation of the lining, which can lead to nephritis, a disorder that can cause permanent kidney damage. Alcohol also causes edema, body fluid retention, and body tissue swelling.

Bladder: Alcohol irritates the lining, and this can develop into cystitis or prostatitis, disorders older adults are already at greater risk for developing. Alcohol decreases resistance to infections and can increase frequency of urination and incontinence.

Liver: Alcohol is responsible for serious problems including jaundice, hepatitis, cirrhosis, low or high blood sugar levels, varicose veins, and increases in cholesterol and fatty acid levels, which lead to fatty liver and gout. Alcohol reduces production of albumin, globulin, and prothrombin, causing loss of fluid in cells, inability to resist infections, and poor blood clotting. An unhealthy liver won't metabolize alcohol out of the body at a normal rate, so alcohol circulates in the bloodstream longer, causing greater damage to all organ systems.

Daily drinking also increases risk for leukemia and lymphoma. Alcoholism causes 75 percent of the cases of cancer of the esophagus and 50 percent of the cases of cancer of the larynx. Drinking also increases the chance of contracting lung, urinary tract, liver, gastric, colorectal, pancreatic, breast, and brain cancer.

Alcoholism causes diarrhea, serious pneumonia, insomnia, hemorrhagic stroke or bleeding in the brain, muscle damage, malnutrition, hypoglycemia, loss of balance, brain damage, and lung failure. In older people, organs can be damaged by a smaller amount of alcohol in the bloodstream.

Long-term heavy drinking causes damage to the cerebral cortex, the area of the brain responsible for abstract thinking and problem solving, verbal skills and memory, and fine and gross motor skills. Katherine Ketcham and William Asbury describe this phenomenon in the book *Beyond the Influence:* "As alcoholism progresses, the brain's ventricles (hollow spaces) enlarge and the cortex shrinks. Brain shrinkage occurs in women with shorter periods of exposure to alcohol. . . . In elderly drinkers, much smaller amounts of alcohol can lead to cognitive impairments, such as mental confusion, memory loss, and perceptual problems, and difficulties with problem solving." A study conducted at the University of Maryland found that 10 percent of patients aged sixty and over who were diagnosed with Alzheimer's disease were actually suffering from brain damage or toxicity caused by alcoholic drinking. As Ketcham and Asbury note, "In alcoholic patients, the brain begins to clear after two months of abstinence; in patients with Alzheimer's, the brain damage is irreversible."

Taking a tour through the organ systems of the body gives us insight into the intricate relationship between alcohol and the health problems of our elder alcoholics. Alcohol affects the body in so many different ways, researchers cannot determine fully the myriad health problems related to alcohol.

Yet, while the symptomatic illnesses grab everyone's attention, the underlying chemical dependency usually goes ignored, undiagnosed, or untreated. Half the medicines prescribed to treat the illnesses caused by alcoholism interact badly with alcohol, causing even more health problems. It becomes an unmanageable downward spiral, and we wrongly chalk it up to old age.

⚓

The Older Adult's Addiction Affects the Health of the Spouse (and Anyone Else Closely Involved)

The stress of living with an alcoholic can seriously affect the health of the entire family. Awareness of this health-diminishing effect upon family members is especially critical for older spouses. They, like older alcoholics, are already more vulnerable to illness because of advancing age. By living with an alcoholic, they lose their good health far sooner than if their mates were not alcoholic, putting them at risk for falling ill and moving into the world of the old-old.

For alcoholics, the drug has a direct impact on the body tissues and organs. This is called *somatic illness,* meaning "affecting the body." The drug is directly changing the organs. For spouses and others, the emotional changes caused by their relationship with the alcoholic directly impact their own tissues and organs. This is called a *psychosomatic illness,* meaning the *psyche* (mind) is changing the *soma* (body). Max A. Schneider, M.D., an internist and gastroenterologist specializing in addiction, clarifies this point:

> This is not imaginary. Psychosomatic illnesses are not just in the head, but are direct changes within the organ systems (the soma) secondary to the emotional disturbances. . . . Many of the same disorders common to alcoholics and drug addicts occur in non-drug using family members. They suffer with many of the same physical and emotional problems as the alcoholic or the drug addict.

Once changes occur in the organ systems, the organs cause changes in our feelings and emotions. This is called *somatopsychic disorder*, meaning the *soma* (body) is changing the *psyche* (emotions). The most obvious examples occur with cerebral changes, which can lead to impaired judgment, depression, anxiety, nervousness, behavior changes, emotional withdrawal, concentration problems, memory loss, fatigue, mood swings, or suicide.

Spouses of older adult alcoholics are at higher risk for diseases such as strokes, hypertension, irregular heartbeat, spastic colon, gastritis, peptic ulcer, colitis, irritable bladder, and many others. Older spouses experience illnesses in the same organ systems as their alcoholic mates do and often suffer the exact same diseases. The psychosomatic illnesses, like the somatic, can be quite serious and at times fatal.

Since the adult children are younger and stronger, they are less susceptible to some of the diseases their parents are at high risk for. It is more likely that they will experience gastrointestinal problems: esophagitis, gastritis, peptic ulcer, irritable bowel syndrome, and colitis. In addition, they are more vulnerable to anxiety disorder, eating disorders, frequent accidents, depression, headaches, sleep deprivation, and memory loss. The wear and tear on their emotions can lead to mood swings that affect their spouses and children. The problem spreads further into the family.

In his video lecture *The Medical Aspects of Co-Dependency,* Dr. Max Schneider makes side-by-side comparisons of the health problems of the alcoholic and the family. The result is eye-opening. With Dr. Schneider's permission, we've created a comparison chart based on his lecture. Notice the similarities between the addicted older person and his or her spouse and children.

How Alcohol and Other Drug Addictions Affect Family Health

Gastrointestinal Diseases

Addicted Older Adult	Spouse and Other Relations
Esophagitis Gastritis Peptic ulcer Pancreatitis Hepatitis	Esophagitis Gastritis Peptic ulcer
Malabsorption Malnutrition	Malabsorption from irritable bowel syndrome Spastic colon or colitis Diarrhea Constipation
Sugar imbalance Secondary diabetes	Eating disorders Bulimia Anorexia Overeating

Cardiovascular Diseases

Addicted Older Adult	Spouse and Other Relations
Hypertension Irregular heartbeat Stroke	Hypertension Irregular heartbeat Stroke

Skeletal Injury

Addicted Older Adult	Spouse and Other Relations
Accidents Fractures Bruises Burns Drowning *Due to impaired judgment caused by the impact alcohol or other drugs have upon the brain*	Accidents Fractures Bruises Burns *Due to impaired judgment caused by preoccupation and worry about the alcoholic and violent outbursts by the alcoholic*

Urinary Tract Diseases

Addicted Older Adult	Spouse and Other Relations
Irritable bladder Urge incontinence	Irritable bladder Urge incontinence Enuresis (bed-wetting)
Prostatitis	

Nervous System/Emotional Disorders

Addicted Older Adult	Spouse and Other Relations
Anxious and nervous Reduced concentration Memory loss Sleep disorders Headaches Impaired judgment Fatigue	Anxious and nervous Reduced concentration Memory loss Sleep disorders Headaches Impaired judgment Fatigue
Denial Begins to hide use, pills, bottles	Denial Begins to cover for or deny the problem
Psychological addiction Physical addiction	Becomes "addicted" to the alcoholic The alcoholic takes center stage
Fears losing the drug Withdrawal	Fears losing their loved one Withdrawal Grief
Depression Suicide	Depression Suicide

Intimacy and Sexuality

Addicted Older Adult	Spouse and Other Relations
Intimacy—feelings are blocked by mood-altering substances	Intimacy—feelings are blocked by shutting down emotionally to avoid pain
Sexual performance—reduced capacity or desire	Sexual performance—reduced capacity or desire
Acting out—inappropriate sexual behavior	Acting out—inappropriate sexual behavior
Hormonal and emotional changes	Hormonal and emotional changes
"Not there"—alcohol has replaced relationships in the alcoholic's life	Grief—feeling the loss of the loved one Loneliness

Addiction is a family disease. No one close to an alcoholic remains unaffected. When the family gets into recovery, many of the medical problems disappear. Health and family relationships improve. Life gets better. Listen to Dr. Schneider: "I have seen recovering people and they are *beautiful.* I have seen recovery and it is *powerful.* It takes effort to accomplish recovery, *but it is worth it.*"

⚓

When Helping Becomes Enabling

When someone we love is in trouble, we rush in to help. That's what people who love each other do. We offer our time, our resources, our empathy. We make things easier in any way we can. But when the trouble is addiction, making things easier is called *enabling.*

No child wants to see a parent deteriorate. No spouse wants to see the person they've shared their life with wither. When the family can't deny the problem any longer, and the aging alcoholic is losing the ability to live independently, everyone in the family reacts differently. We've seen many "solutions" put in place by family members. A spouse attempts to control the drinking by doling out a daily alcohol ration. An adult child goes through the house locating hidden bottles and pouring them out. Everyone in the family takes turns baby-sitting the alcoholic so she doesn't drink herself to death or burn the house down. They clean the house, buy her groceries, pay her bills—keep everything as it was before the addiction took over. All of these "solutions" require tremendous energy and sacrifice. None of them solves the problem.

It is not uncommon for elder spouses to resist dealing directly with the alcoholism of their mates. There are several reasons for this. First, older adults were raised to believe that you do not "air your dirty laundry," but rather solve your problems privately. They are not part of the self-help generation and resist therapy and support groups. They avoid burdening their children with their problems. In addition, the disease of alcoholism is seen as a weakness of character rather than an illness. Therefore, it has a pronounced stigma to many in this age group.

Adult children usually get involved when serious problems begin to surface. Below are examples of behaviors that endanger the alcoholic's safety or the safety of others:

- driving drunk
- passing out with a cigarette burning or food cooking
- wandering outside at night disoriented and intoxicated
- developing serious health and/or cognitive problems
- becoming unable to live alone and care for himself
- threatening to commit suicide

As the addiction worsens, the nonalcoholic parent is often unwilling to find outside help for the alcoholic. The grown children are left to produce a plan that will initiate treatment for their alcoholic parent.

Dr. Jerry Boriskin, a psychologist specializing in addictions, says:

> It has been said that living with or around an alcoholic or addict is like watching a train wreck in slow motion. In order to cope and to stave off helplessness, the adult children's first reflex is to deny and minimize the problem: *This isn't happening. This isn't real. Mom's always been in control. Dad's my Rock of Gibraltar.* Seeing behaviors in Mom or Dad that don't make sense sets off huge emotional triggers in adult children. To cope, they frequently revert to old family roles and dynamics.

These old roles are often adapted into enabling roles designed to contain the damage caused by the addiction.

We can identify three primary *enabling roles* adult children use as a way of coping with an aging parent's addiction: *Rescuer*, *Scolder*, and *Concealer*. In large sibling groups, more than one person may take on the same enabling role. In small sibling groups, a person may take on more than one role. Each of these roles is intended to make a bad situation better. But, unwittingly, each helps keep the addiction in place.

The Rescuer is the sibling who anticipates every problem and tries to solve it before it happens. For instance, Mom might fall at night while she's intoxicated, so the Rescuer moves her into the downstairs bedroom, removes all the area rugs, and installs night-lights in the hallways and bathrooms. The Rescuer keeps Mom's house tidy, gets the laundry done, and cooks a week's worth of dinners to keep in the freezer. She knows where Mom hides all of her bottles and regularly goes on a raid, emptying them all down the drain.

When Mom is at her worst, the Rescuer cleans her up and doesn't mention it to the rest of the family. She pumps her full of vitamins and feeds her something nourishing. She takes time off work, rearranges schedules, and spends less and less time with her husband and children. She drops what she's doing at a moment's notice when she gets a distress call from Mom. She is the primary caregiver. She often denies alcohol is the real problem. She believes that the problem is Mom's grief over Dad's death, her loneliness, and the many difficulties Mom's faced throughout her life. The Rescuer exerts tremendous energy doing the best job she can to keep her mother safe and well cared for. Everything the Rescuer does is very important for a dependent, aging parent. But when the older parent is alcoholic, it does not replace treating the alcoholism. It would be as if an aging parent were suffering from cancer, and you made her as comfortable as possible but never took her to the oncologist.

The Rescuer never directly addresses the cause of the endless, unsolvable problems—alcoholism. She keeps secrets and fixes problems as fast as they happen, so no one sees a clear picture of the severity of Mom's problem. The Rescuer protects herself from feelings of fear and helplessness by *always being in control.* She resents her siblings for not helping out more, but she rarely asks for help. No matter how long and hard she works to control the problem, the alcoholism is always one step ahead of her. In the long run, her mom gets worse. The Rescuer burns out. Her family suffers. Only the alcoholism prevails.

The Scolder is the sibling who is angry and resentful. She complains that the Rescuer coddles Mom. "If she can't take care of herself, too bad," the thinking goes. "Maybe she'll wake up and take control of her life once no one is taking care of everything for her." The Scolder and the Rescuer often clash. The Scolder shames, chastises, and nags her mom or gives her the cold shoulder and doesn't call or visit. The Scolder understands that alcoholism is the problem and lets everybody know it. She expects her mom to "get her act together," and when she doesn't, she punishes her. Of course, "getting it together" is an unrealistic expectation for an alcoholic who is suffering from a disease marked by loss of control.

The Scolder's anger originates from fear, frustration, and hurt. To the Scolder, Mom's alcoholism feels like *something her mom is doing to her* rather than *something that is happening to Mom.* She protects herself by showing anger rather than vulnerability. The Scolder allows the disease to flourish by wrongly expecting her mom to overcome the problem on her own without a proper treatment and recovery program.

The Concealer never really talks to his mom about her drinking problem, but he indirectly lets her know he's disappointed and ashamed of her. The Concealer is embarrassed by his mother's alcoholism. He withdraws from the family. He avoids seeing his mom and discourages others from talking about her alcoholism. He shames his mother by using indirect, nonverbal communication. He sees her as a bad person, not a sick person. He believes her alcoholism reflects poorly on the whole family. The Concealer tries to maintain the status quo.

He conceals the problem from the outside world and, in doing so, protects his inner world. The Concealer feels abandoned by his addicted parent. He protects himself through avoidance and cover-ups, allowing the alcoholism to flourish. The Concealer clashes with the Scolder because she talks so openly about the drinking problem. The Concealer depends on the Rescuer so he doesn't have to deal with the problem directly. The Rescuer resents the Concealer because she feels he's left the work up to her while he retreats into his own life.

Each of these enabling roles has two goals: (1) minimizing the damage caused by the alcoholism and (2) protecting the adult children from the emotional pain they are experiencing. None of the enabling roles deals directly with the addiction, only with the symptoms of the addiction. These roles keep the adult children from cooperating with each other. Rescuers, Scolders, and Concealers don't mix. They clash. Adult children must drop their enabling roles so they can unite and work together on the real problem: chemical dependency.

Some methods used to stop the enabling process are not appropriate for many older adults. We often hear about tough love or letting the alcoholic hit bottom. These terms refer to standing back and not helping the alcoholic in any way. In doing so, the consequences come crashing down around the alcoholic and, one hopes, motivate him to reach out for help. This hard-line approach is often not advisable for aging alcoholics, especially when they are unable to care for themselves. For an older person, hitting bottom often means death.

Learning not to enable the disease of addiction requires education and loving honesty. Don't do what the alcoholic can do for himself. Stop managing the problem. Focus on solutions instead. Learn the right way to help your aging parent recover from his disease. Don't clean up all the messes. Separate out healthy caregiving from enabling. Get support for yourself. Attend a Twelve Step group for families of alcoholics and find a caregivers support group. Check your phone book for listings, call your local agency on aging, or locate online meetings. Resources at the back of this book will help point you in the right direction.

⚜

Ignoring the Problem Can Preserve the Problem

Enabling makes it easier for alcoholics to stay in their disease. When other people *enable* or cover for them, alcoholics don't experience the consequences of their addiction. Consequences are signals that tell them something is wrong. Denial, the hallmark of chemical dependency, is strengthened when consequences are lessened. Alcoholics don't see drinking as a problem; drinking is desirable. Enablers are desirable, too. They make drinking easier. When we ignore the problem, *it's what we don't do* that defines our enabling.

Overlooking addiction is easiest in the lives of aging alcoholics. Retired, they are not facing job loss or workplace intervention. If the spouse is living, it is less likely he or she will divorce the alcoholic spouse at this stage in life. If the spouse has passed away, alcoholics often find alcoholic companions who encourage a drinking life. Older alcoholics drink at home much of the time, avoiding legal problems such as driving under the influence. They also don't have problems associated with illegal drugs since most get drugs prescribed by doctors. Since older alcoholics aren't raising children, employed, or driving as much, the alcoholism is less likely to get in other people's way. It is more easily ignored.

Many of the consequences older people experience are related to health, social activities, nutrition, and family life, and they are attributed to aging. The alcohol is viewed as a peripheral part of the whole picture rather than the lead player. To determine the alcohol-related consequences your older relative is experiencing, turn to the resource section at the back of the book and take the quiz "Signs of Alcoholism and Drug Abuse in Older People."

Eleanor was a social butterfly at seventy-one years old. She was attractive, energetic, financially independent, and active. She golfed, played bridge, traveled the world, threw endless dinner parties for her many friends, and enjoyed the company of gentlemen eager to wine and dine her. Although Eleanor had a long history of alcoholism and medication addiction, she hid her problems from her children. She wintered in Florida, making it easy to live a double life. She used caller ID to screen her children's calls when she was intoxicated.

Although the kids all knew she had a problem, they ignored Eleanor's addiction because it wasn't evident most of the time. Nor was it intruding upon their lives. When a cousin recounted how Eleanor, driving a golf cart with drink in hand, overturned the cart, throwing Eleanor's eighty-year-old sister to the ground, everyone chuckled and ignored the obvious. After all, no harm was done. Both sisters walked away unhurt.

Eleanor's best friend was an alcoholic, and her entire social circle consisted of heavy drinkers, so none of her friends was alarmed when she overimbibed. In fact, this group was intolerant of anyone who didn't drink. No one wanted a nondrinker around to make the rest of them look like a bunch of lushes. So Eleanor fit right into the crowd.

Although Eleanor seemed at the top of her game, she suffered from several health problems related to alcoholism: heart arrhythmia, high blood pressure, depression, edema, insomnia, diarrhea, and irritable bladder. Her doctors prescribed a medication for each, but never broached the topic of alcoholism.

Knowing that each of these diseases can be caused by alcohol, all of them together should have been a red flag. The doctors enabled Eleanor by prescribing medications to treat the problems secondary to alcoholism, but never addressing the alcoholism itself.

Eleanor's doctors prescribed antidepressants, high blood pressure medication, diuretics, heartbeat stabilizers, tranquilizers, sleeping pills, and antidiarrhea medication. She also took over-the-counter sleep and weight-loss medications. Eleanor's philosophy about medication was this: If one is good, two are better. Doctor's orders were brushed aside like unwelcome advice. She manipulated her medications to get a desired effect. If a medication didn't act fast enough or give Eleanor the result she wanted, she took more.

Taking her medications with alcohol put Eleanor at serious risk. The antidepressant mixed with alcohol resulted in increased depression. The drug used to reduce her edema (body fluid retention) increased the intoxicating effect of alcohol. Her high blood pressure medications mixed with alcohol could cause a dangerous drop in blood pressure. With alcohol, the medication to stabilize her irregular heartbeat could further depress her normal heart function. Mixing sleeping pills with alcohol increased the sedation effect of both. Diarrhea medication increased the intoxicating effect of alcohol, and alcohol increased the diarrhea. Eleanor mixed all these medications with alcohol every day.

One night, nervous about a big date, Eleanor tripled her heart medication to calm herself. At the restaurant, she started with a martini and then drank wine with the main course. By dessert, she was passed out on the floor. When the paramedics arrived, Eleanor had no heartbeat. In the hospital, when Eleanor regained consciousness, her doctors recommended immediate open-heart surgery to install a pacemaker. She protested, but the doctors insisted. It was a lifesaving procedure, they said. Finally, not knowing how else to refuse the surgery, she admitted to her overuse of medications and alcohol.

Her close brush with death alarmed and worried her children. But once the crisis was over and Eleanor was back to "normal," nobody examined the problem further. Sure, everyone chastised her for not following her doctor's orders, but the overuse of medication was treated as "a silly thing Mom does." Eleanor was perceived as incorrigible, but no one talked about alcoholism and medication abuse. Eleanor's grown children all enabled her by obeying the no-talk rules put in place years earlier—the children knew not talk to each other, to their mother, or to any relative or friend about her alcohol and medication problems.

Ask yourself these questions to determine if you've enabled an elder alcoholic to stay addicted by ignoring the problem. Have you

- Denied or made excuses to family and friends to hide the alcohol or medication addiction?
- Given the alcoholic permission to drink at certain times, in certain amounts, or on special days?
- Cancelled family plans to hide the problem?
- Encouraged family and friends to ignore the problem?
- Accepted blame for the drinking?
- Downplayed the seriousness of the problem or laughed it off?
- Told other family members it's none of their business when they tried talking about their concerns?
- Used ageism, such as the idea that "at his age, it doesn't matter that he likes to drink," to excuse the drinking or medication abuse? Or said, "She's too old to change," excusing everyone from acting responsibly?

Enabling is a common response to addiction. Enabling the disease by ignoring it is a form of family denial. As we are reminded in the daily meditation book *Courage to Change: One Day at a Time in Al-Anon II*: "As my denial began to lift, I was horrified at the lies I had told myself and others. . . . But I can forgive my extreme responses to extreme situations, knowing that I did the best I could at the time. Today I can be honest and still be gentle with myself."

Alcohol, Prescription Drugs, and Addiction

Chemical Dependency Is a Disease

Chemical dependency is a disease. The American Medical Association made it official in 1956. *Scientific American* first reported alcoholism as a disease in 1877. Documented as far back as Roman times, alcoholism has been identified as an illness. This is not a new thought by scientists and medical professionals, but alcoholism as a disease is difficult to reconcile with the erroneous belief that chemical dependency results from a lack of willpower.

To better understand chemical dependency as a disease, let's take a look at what makes something a disease. *Merriam-Webster's Medical Dictionary* defines *disease* as "an impairment of the normal state of the living animal or plant body or one of its parts that interrupts or modifies the performance of the vital functions and is a response to environmental factors (as malnutrition, industrial hazards, or climate) . . . to inherent defects of the organism (as genetic anomalies), or to combinations of these factors." According to *Encyclopedia Britannica,* sharp demarcation between disease and health is not always apparent.

When we consider any disease, three questions usually come to mind: What are the symptoms? What caused it? How do we cure it? It's not necessary to have the answers to these questions before a condition can be classified as a disease. Symptoms do not always appear in a disease's early stages, and we do not know what causes many diseases, nor can we cure all diseases. Diabetes and Alzheimer's disease are examples. So is chemical dependency.

Etiology is the term we use to describe the causes of diseases. For some illnesses, we know exactly what causes them. For instance, if you have sickle-cell anemia, it's known with certainty that your disease has been caused by a gene inherited from both parents. Not all diseases have such clear-cut etiology.

Many inherited diseases require stimulus from the environment in order to be activated. A perfect illustration of the interrelationship between the environment and genetics is the disease phenylketonuria (PKU). Understanding the dynamics of PKU can help us better understand the disease of chemical dependency.

A child born with PKU has inherited a defective gene from each parent. PKU once caused severe mental retardation, but that is no longer the case because medical science now understands the environment's role in initiating the disease. PKU is activated only after genetically affected children consume *phenylalanine,* an essential amino acid. To avoid the onset of the disease, a child with PKU must simply avoid phenylalanine. A simple change in the environment halts a serious genetic disease.

Chemical dependency, like PKU, is also a genetic and environmental disease. Genes influencing a predisposition to the disease are thought to be inherited from one or both parents. But the environment plays the key role in initiating the disease. Consuming alcohol or other mind-altering drugs is required to activate the disease. People who never drink, but are genetically wired for chemical dependency, never develop the disease. The National Institute on Alcohol Abuse and Alcoholism (NIAAA) recommends that people with a family history of alcoholism abstain from using alcohol. It is the only known way to avoid becoming alcoholic. If there's a possibility you've inherited alcoholic genes, the change must come from your environment—*the decision not to drink.*

We often ascribe a lack of willpower to people suffering from alcoholism. We point to the many drinkers who aren't alcoholic as if to say, "These people are nonalcoholic because they drink responsibly." Many adult children of alcoholics who drink tell themselves, "I'll never be an alcoholic like my father." They believe alcoholism is a choice, and they can drink as long as they *choose* not to be alcoholic. But once an alcoholic starts drinking alcohol, the brain disorder of impaired control takes over. We accept the fact that phenylalanine has a different effect on the small percentage of the population suffering from PKU, but we have difficulty accepting the same of alcohol.

Some diseases can't be cured, but can be controlled. We can delay or avoid the fatality associated with the illness through proper treatment. Sometimes the success of treatment hinges upon patients making changes in their environment or lifestyle. Certainly, a heart bypass patient is given instructions for a heart-healthy diet and regular exercise. If the patient continues to indulge in high-fat foods and never exercises, the next heart attack doesn't mean the bypass failed. When an alcoholic refuses to go to Alcoholics Anonymous after treatment, a relapse doesn't mean treatment failed.

Treating diabetes requires patient compliance, and this is similar to alcoholism in some ways. Insulin is essential for managing some diabetes, but success also requires lifestyle changes—diet, weight control, exercise, monitoring blood glucose several times a day, checking blood pressure, regular medical tests and doctor visits, and a generally healthy lifestyle. When diabetes patients comply with treatment and lifestyle changes, they are less likely to suffer serious complications. When they don't comply, they risk heart disease, stroke, high blood pressure, blindness, amputations, kidney failure, and other life-threatening events. Even under the threat of these devastating consequences, lack of compliance is a common problem among diabetic patients. Compliance problems with diabetics can help us understand the same phenomena with alcoholics.

Successful treatment of chemical dependency hinges primarily upon patient compliance. Although the disease is incurable, when patients comply with an ongoing program of recovery, treatment for chemical dependency has the highest rate of success of any chronic illness. Working the Twelve Steps of Alcoholics Anonymous is the "insulin" for long-term recovery.

Success, as for diabetes, requires lifestyle changes. These include attending Twelve Step meetings several times a week, eating a healthy diet, managing stress, avoiding drinking activities and drinking buddies, learning how to accept help from others, and developing a balanced emotional life. When people make these changes, they have low incidences of relapse. When they don't comply, the risk of relapse rises sharply. Chemically dependent patients, like diabetics, are highly responsible for the success of their treatment. Many alcoholics, who are often in denial about their illness, block recovery through noncompliance.

Alcoholism is a complex disease associated with multiple abnormal genes. Genetic studies estimate that 40 to 60 percent of the vulnerability for chemical dependency is genetically based. The NIAAA Collaborative Study on the Genetics of Alcoholism has identified several sites in the brain where the genes for alcoholism may be located, and the map of the human genome is expected to eventually lead researchers to the many genes responsible for alcoholism. To stay abreast of the recent research into the genetic causes of alcoholism and alcohol-related behavior, go to the Web site for the NIAAA. Request their free publication *Alcohol Alert*. For Web and mailing addresses, turn to the resource section of this book.

Evidence That Alcoholism Is Genetic

Some people may ask: "If we haven't located the responsible genes, can we say with certainty that chemical dependency is genetic? Or is this just a well-educated guess?" Dr. Robert Karp, program director for genetics at the NIAAA, answers, "Even though researchers have not located the genes responsible for alcoholism, there is an overwhelming amount of evidence that alcoholism is inherited."

Many diseases are known to be genetic, but the responsible genes have not been found. Researchers have other methods of studying diseases to determine if they are genetic. Some of the most reliable data on the genetics of alcoholism comes from studies on twins and adoption. Both ask the questions: "Is it nature or nurture? Is it learned or inherited? Or is it both?" These studies have shown reliable and valid results and have been successfully replicated over the years.

Twin studies are based on the hypothesis that if alcoholism is inherited, identical twins would show a similar propensity toward alcoholism, and fraternal twins would show more deviation. This is because identical twins have identical genes, and fraternal twins have some genes that are different. If alcoholism were genetic, each of the identical twins would be equally vulnerable to the disease. Fraternal twins would be more likely to have one alcoholic twin and one nonalcoholic twin. However, if alcoholism were learned, twins growing up in the same environment would be equally influenced by alcoholic parents or caregivers. It wouldn't make any difference if the twins were fraternal or identical. The environment would be the deciding factor, not the genes.

Twin studies have found, again and again, that there is a difference between identical and fraternal twins. If one identical twin is alcoholic, the other is highly likely to be alcoholic. This is not the case for fraternal twins. Fraternal twins are more apt to have one alcoholic and one nonalcoholic twin as compared to identical twins.

Adoption studies, such as one by Donald Goodwin and colleagues in 1978, have compared babies born of alcoholic birth parents and babies born of nonalcoholic birth parents. The babies from both groups were adopted at birth by nonalcoholic couples. If alcoholism is learned, both groups of babies should have similarly low alcoholism rates *regardless of their birth parents' histories of alcoholism* because they were raised in nonalcoholic homes. But this is not the case. As adults, adopted babies with an alcoholic birth parent are four times more likely to develop alcoholism than are babies from nonalcoholic birth parents.

A Swedish study by C. R. Cloninger et al., reported in 1981, combined twin and adoption studies. Researchers followed twin pairs who were adopted into separate homes and raised apart from one another. Twin pairs with alcoholic birth parents had a dramatically higher incidence of alcoholism than twin pairs born of nonalcoholic parents. Since each individual twin was raised in a different home, the similar propensity toward alcoholism points to genes rather than environment.

Animal studies also point to the hereditary nature of alcoholism. Using mice and other animals, researchers can study alcoholism using larger numbers of subjects and multiple generations. They can also control mating activities and the environment. These controls cannot be imposed upon humans.

Mice have been genetically altered to have different sensitivities to alcohol. One group was sensitive to alcohol; the other was less sensitive. Alcohol-sensitive mice have a low tolerance for alcohol. After consuming alcohol, their behaviors change quickly and they pass out sooner. Alcohol-desensitized mice have a higher tolerance for alcohol. They can drink for longer periods of time before their behavior changes or before they pass out. Having less sensitivity to alcohol is linked to a higher risk for alcoholism. We often describe the alcohol-desensitized person as the one who can "drink everyone else under the table."

In other studies, mice have been genetically engineered to be alcohol-preferring or alcohol-avoiding mice. Alcohol-preferring mice chose alcohol over water. Alcohol-avoiding mice avoided drinking alcohol even when deprived of water. When bred, alcohol-preferring mice produced alcohol-preferring offspring; alcohol-avoiding mice produced offspring that avoided alcohol.

Researchers have successfully bred mice with high or low incidences of the following alcohol-related behaviors: sedation, loss of physical coordination, euphoria, withdrawal symptoms, and tolerance of the different effects of alcohol. Studying genetically altered mice indicates that, although both environment and genetics affect alcoholism, genes may have the greater influence.

While these studies do not pinpoint which genes are linked to alcoholism, they do present a broad view of the genetic influence on this disease. But, as stated by Dr. Enoch Gordis, the director of the NIAAA, "These genes are for risk, not for destiny." No single factor causes alcoholism. However, for those who choose to drink alcohol, genetic vulnerability tips the balance in favor of alcoholism.

⚟

Alcoholism Begins at Any Age

Chemical dependency shows up at different times in different people. Some people become alcoholic in their teens, others in midlife, and still others in their senior years. A person drinks without problems for decades before becoming alcoholic while another is alcoholic from his first drink. Chemical dependency, as with other diseases, affects different people at different times in their lives. We identify alcoholism in three ways: *early, late,* and *periodic onset.*

Two-thirds of chemically dependent older adults suffer from *early onset* alcoholism. They usually became alcoholic somewhere between the ages of fourteen and twenty-five. Throughout their lives, they have turned to alcohol to cope with problems, to feel less inhibited in social situations, and to feel comfortable with themselves. As the alcoholic drinking patterns continue, they drink just to satisfy the alcoholism. Early onset is characterized by a family history of alcoholism, chronic alcohol-related medical problems such as cirrhosis, organic brain syndrome (physical conditions that cause a decrease in mental function), depression, or other disorders. Early onset alcoholics are unsuccessful agers. They adjust poorly to the changes that come with old age, they have more health problems and family problems, and they make repeated, unhealthy life decisions. Alcoholism blocks their ability to grow into this new stage in their lives.

One-third of older adult alcoholics suffer from *late onset* alcoholism. They never had problems with alcohol or other drugs before the age of fifty-five or sixty. Alcoholism was triggered late in life, precipitated by increased drinking in response to life changes or losses. In other cases, older adults drink the same amount as they always have, but their aging bodies react as if they are drinking more. Older adults might also mix alcohol with over-the-counter or prescription mood-altering drugs. In each of these scenarios, the amount of alcohol became sufficient to trip the genetic wiring for alcoholism.

Having a shorter history with the disease, late onset alcoholics are healthier than early onset alcoholics. Therefore, health care professionals are more likely to overlook their alcohol dependence. But, like early onset alcoholics, late onset alcoholics use alcohol almost daily, in most social situations, when home alone, and as a way to self-medicate. Seeing their addiction as an age-related problem, older adults who develop alcoholism late in life are usually more agreeable to treatment than early onset alcoholics. Here's an example of how late onset alcoholism played out in one woman's life.

Ruth was never much of a drinker. She had five kids to raise and a house to keep. She couldn't remember ever drinking too much. Ruth rarely had time for alcohol.

When Ruth's husband retired, they sold the big family house and moved to a Florida retirement community. Life was geared toward leisure activities with other retirees. Alcohol was a prominent part of the fun. Ruth and her husband always joined in by having two or three drinks a night. In a matter of a few months, Ruth went from drinking fewer than ten glasses of wine a year to as many as fifteen a week.

Three years later, Ruth's husband had a fatal stroke. As a widow, Ruth's life changed. She stayed active during the day, but stopped going out in the evenings. Home alone, her grief overwhelmed her. She was lonely and afraid. When she tried to sleep, she couldn't. To quiet her nerves, she began drinking alone at night.

Soon, Ruth began complaining of constant pain. Medical examinations and tests revealed nothing. Doctors didn't consider that Ruth's pain might be a symptom of her grief. Ruth was *somatizing* her grief—experiencing her emotional pain as physical pain. She needed grief counseling, but instead got a narcotic analgesic pain medication. Ruth was told not to mix the medication with alcohol, so she took pain pills during the day and drank at night.

Insomnia continued to plague Ruth. She discussed it with her doctor, and he prescribed sleeping pills. Ruth continued to take pain pills during the day, drink wine in the evenings, and take sleeping medication at night. She felt sure she was following her doctor's orders and not mixing alcohol with her medications.

Ruth's children began noticing bruises on her legs, arms, and face. They were concerned when she forgot conversations and appeared confused. They worried because she wasn't paying bills on time and had two minor car accidents in six months. They decided she was too old to take care of herself and started looking for an assisted-living facility. It didn't occur to them that their mother, who rarely took a drink in the first sixty years of her life, was suffering from the life-threatening disease of chemical dependency. Once they understood that addiction was her primary problem, they talked with her doctor and intervened.

When her children asked her to get treatment, Ruth told them she knew she had a problem, but she didn't know what to do about it. She achieved sobriety through a recovery program for alcoholism. With recovery, most of her health problems disappeared.

The following chart is adapted from *Substance Abuse among Older Adults,* published by the U.S. Department of Health and Human Services. It differentiates between the characteristics of early and late onset alcoholism:

Variable	Early Onset	Late Onset
Typical age at onset	14 to 25, but can vary with ages as late as 45	Over 55; as late as 60s and 70s
Gender	Higher proportion of men than women	Higher proportion of women than men
Drinking in response to stress	Common	Common
Extent and severity of alcohol problems	More psychosocial & legal problems, greater severity	Fewer psychosocial & legal problems, lesser severity
Alcohol-related chronic illness (cirrhosis, pancreatitis, cancer)	More common	Less common
Psychiatric comorbidities	Cognitive loss more severe, less reversible	Cognitive loss less severe, more reversible
Age-associated medical problems aggravated by alcohol (hypertension, diabetes, drug interactions)	Common	Common
Breakdown of elderly alcoholics/addicts	Two-thirds	One-third
Tolerance to alcohol and other drugs	Increased, then decreased	Decreased

Variable	Early Onset	Late Onset
Motivation to accept treatment	Fear of loss of job, loss of family, and serious health problems	Fear of serious health problems, injury, family and social problems
Intervention methods	Legal system, physician, family, workplace	Family and friends, physician, caregivers
Treatment compliance and outcome	Possibly less compliant; relapse rates do not vary by age of onset	Possibly more compliant; relapse rates do not vary by age of onset

Periodic onset alcoholics drink during different times in their lives and not during others. Problems usually start in their twenties, but they successfully stop drinking for varying lengths of time throughout their lives. Following periods of abstinence that can last for years, heavy drinking returns. Regardless of how long a periodic onset alcoholic abstains from drinking, relapse can happen at any age. Older adults suffering from periodic onset are at higher risk for relapse when they experience grief, loss, or loneliness. Maureen is an example. She drank heavily in her twenties, but after she had children, she stopped drinking. Once her children were grown, she started again. Quickly, she began showing symptoms of alcoholism—blacking out, slurred speech, personality changes, mood swings. This went on for a few years until her husband threatened to divorce her if she didn't quit drinking. So she quit again. But Maureen resumed drinking when her husband died.

Binge drinking is a pattern of use. It is defined in *Substance Abuse among Older Adults* as "short periods of loss of control over drinking alternating with periods of abstinence or much lighter alcohol use. . . . A *binge* itself is usually defined as any drinking occasion in which an individual consumes five or more standard drinks." A binge for older adults is four or more drinks on a single occasion. Binge drinking is different than periodic onset. A binge is a pattern of drinking not associated with onset.

Binge drinkers can be early, late, or periodic onset alcoholics. Older adult binge drinkers are harder to identify because they leave less evidence, such as drunk driving arrests. Young adults who are binge drinkers usually age into continuous, daily drinkers in late life.

Some older adults experience *idiosyncratic intoxication*—they become drunk from small amounts of alcohol that would not intoxicate most people. This indicates a diminished tolerance to alcohol possibly caused by advanced age. Wrongly believing that alcoholism is determined by the amount of alcohol consumed, a family can overlook an older relative's problem if he's only having one or two drinks a night. But each drink may affect the older adult as though he's had five or six. If an older adult is having negative consequences that are consistent with alcoholism, he may have a problem regardless of the amount he drinks.

To order a free copy of *Substance Abuse among Older Adults*, published by the U.S. Department of Health and Human Services, contact the National Clearinghouse for Alcohol and Drug Information at 800-729-6686 and ask for TIP 26. Order an extra copy for the older adult's primary care physician.

⚏

Identifying Alcoholism and Prescription Drug Abuse

Chemical dependency is a disease with predictable symptoms. It continuously gets worse over time if left untreated and is incurable. It is characterized by an increased tolerance—needing more to get the same effect—and periodic loss of control over the drug.

The American Society of Addiction Medicine and the National Council on Alcoholism and Drug Dependence define alcoholism as "a primary chronic disease with genetic, psychosocial, and environmental manifestations. The disease is often progressive and fatal. It is characterized by impaired control over drinking, preoccupation with the drug alcohol, use of alcohol despite adverse consequences, and a distortion in thinking, most notably denial."

When the focus is solely on the aging population, the American Medical Association expands this definition to say, "The onset or continuation of drinking behavior that becomes problematic because of physiological and psychological changes that occur with aging, including increased sensitivity to alcohol effects."

The first step in determining whether an older adult has an alcohol or medication problem is by talking to her. Using non-threatening language is important because many older adults view alcoholism as a moral failing and think of alcoholics as skid-row bums. Avoid the words *alcoholic* or *alcoholism* and use *alcohol problem* instead. Questions such as "Is alcohol causing you problems?" "Do you notice side effects when you have a drink?" "Are there times when you think the alcohol affected you more than you expected?" show empathy for the older adult's well-being rather than focusing on problem drinking. Ask similar questions about medications: "Do you find you need to take more sleeping pills before they begin working for you?" Stay away from blame, anger, and judgment. Have this conversation when the older adult is sober. If she admits that alcohol or drugs are causing problems, ask if she'd be willing to see a doctor about how alcohol and medications affect older bodies. To find a doctor with special training in addiction, contact the American Society of Addiction Medicine at 301-656-3920 and ask to speak with the membership assistant, or e-mail nbrig@asam.org.

Doctors have several tools for assessing chemical dependency. Assessment and screening tests collect information about drinking behaviors and related problems. The Michigan Alcoholism Screening Test—Geriatric Version, commonly called the

MAST-G, is the most frequently used test for older adults. Ask the doctor to administer the MAST-G when assessing your older relative. If the doctor doesn't have a copy of the test available, offer to fax a copy to his or her office. The test is royalty-free, so doctors don't pay to use it. A word of caution: *Do not administer this test yourself.* Using it as "proof" of alcoholism can shame the alcoholic, create resentment, and close doors to communication. Older adults are more likely to respond openly and honestly to a trusted doctor. A doctor trained in addiction medicine will present results appropriately and make treatment recommendations as necessary.

Michigan Alcoholism Screening Test — Geriatric Version

☐ After drinking, have you ever noticed an increase in your heart rate or beating in your chest?

☐ When talking with others, do you ever underestimate how much you actually drink?

☐ Does alcohol make you sleepy so that you fall asleep in your chair?

☐ After a few drinks, have you sometimes not eaten or skipped a meal because you didn't feel hungry?

☐ Does having a few drinks help decrease your shakiness or tremors?

☐ Does alcohol sometimes make it hard for you to remember parts of the day or night?

☐ Do you have rules for yourself that you won't drink before a certain time of the day?

☐ Have you lost interest in hobbies or activities you used to enjoy?

☐ When you wake up in the morning, do you ever have trouble remembering part of the night before?

☐ Does having a drink help you sleep?

☐ Do you hide your alcohol bottles from family members?

☐ After a social gathering, have you ever felt embarrassed because you drank too much?

☐ Have you ever been concerned that drinking might be harmful to your health?

☐ Do you like to end an evening with a nightcap?

☐ Did you find your drinking increased after someone close to you died?

☐ In general, would you prefer to have a few drinks at home rather than go out to a social event?

☐ Are you drinking more now than in the past?

☐ Do you usually take a drink to relax or calm your nerves?

☐ Do you drink to take your mind off your problems?

☐ Have you ever increased your drinking after experiencing a loss in your life?

☐ Do you sometimes drive when you've had too much to drink?

☐ Has a doctor or nurse ever said they were worried or concerned about your drinking?

☐ Have you ever made rules to manage your drinking?

☐ When you feel lonely, does it help to have a drink?

Scoring: Five or more yes responses is indicative of an alcohol problem.

For further information, contact Frederic Blow, Ph.D., at the University of Michigan Alcohol Research Center, 400 East Eisenhower Parkway, Suite A, Ann Arbor, MI 48104, 734-998-7952. Copyright 1991 the Regents of the University of Michigan.

A shorter screening test, valid for older adults, is the CAGE Questionnaire, developed in 1970 by Dr. John Ewing. It consists of only four questions. It can be altered to screen for mood-altering prescription drugs by replacing the word *drinking* with the name of the offending drug. Doctors should use it in conjunction with interviews with family members, thorough physical exams, and laboratory tests.

The CAGE Questionnaire

1. Have you ever felt you should **cut down** on your drinking?
2. Have people **annoyed** you by criticizing your drinking?
3. Have you ever felt bad or **guilty** about your drinking?
4. Have you ever had a drink first thing in the morning to steady your nerves or to get rid of a hangover **(eye-opener)**?

Each no answer is given the score of 0, and each yes answer is given a score of 1. A total score of 2 or more indicates that the probability of alcoholism is high.

The American Medical Association recommends that doctors look for multiple signs when diagnosing alcoholism. If there are several positive signs, there's a high probability for chemical dependency. The following is a list of physical symptoms the American Medical Association suggests doctors look for:

- bruises, abrasions, and scars in locations that might suggest frequent falls, bumping into objects, physical altercations, or other violent behavior
- cigarette burns on the fingers
- flushed or florid faces (a thin face with sunken eyeballs, sallow complexion, and yellow conjunctivae) and other dermatological involvement
- nystagmus or amblyopia (jerky eye movement or loss of central vision)
- peripheral neuropathy (damage to nerves causing numbness and tingling)
- hypertension, particularly systolic (pressure exerted when the heart contracts)
- gastrointestinal or other bleeding
- cirrhosis or other evidence of liver impairment, such as edema in the lower extremities, ascites (excess fluid in the abdomen), and other signs of fluid retention
- psoriasis and signs of immunodeficient disorders

The Center for Substance Abuse Treatment identifies additional physical symptoms to consider when screening for alcoholism:

- sleep complaints, observable changes in sleep patterns, unusual fatigue, malaise, daytime drowsiness, apparent sedation (for example, a formerly punctual older adult begins oversleeping)
- seizures, malnutrition, muscle wasting
- depression and/or anxiety
- unexplained complaints about chronic pain or other somatic complaints
- incontinence, urinary retention, difficulty urinating
- poor hygiene and self-neglect
- unusual restlessness or agitation
- complaints of blurred vision or dry mouth
- unexplained nausea and vomiting or gastrointestinal distress
- changes in eating habits
- slurred speech
- tremor, motor uncoordination, shuffling gait

Ask the older adult's doctor to look, during the physical exam, for these signs associated with chemical dependency. Blood tests can help determine chronic heavy drinking, but only when used as a supplement to screening questionnaires and history-taking interviews. Abnormal lab values tend to be more common in alcoholics over age sixty-four, but not every older alcoholic shows abnormal blood chemistry.

When assessing for alcoholism, doctors should evaluate cognitive functioning. If a patient is positive for cognitive impairment, the doctor should consider alcoholism as one of the possible causes. The American Medical Association recommends that doctors compare a patient's cognitive functioning to other patients of the same age who are not alcoholic. They list several symptoms alcoholics exhibit:

- severe recent memory loss
- inability to concentrate
- defensiveness or irritation when asked even routine, general questions about alcohol use
- extreme mood swings, even during a single office visit
- undue concern about physical ailments, sometimes bordering on hypochondria
- suicidal ideation

A doctor's evaluation of the older adult's cognitive status can be further evaluated by administering the Mini-Mental Status Exam (MMSE).

Every older adult should be screened for alcohol and prescription drug abuse during his regular physical exam according to the Substance Abuse and Mental Health Services Administration. If your older relative's doctor is untrained in assessing older adults for alcoholism, recommend the American Medical Association's publication *Alcoholism in the Elderly: Diagnosis, Treatment, Prevention*. It is available by writing to the Department of Geriatric Health, American Medical Association, 515 North State Street, Chicago, IL 60610; or call 312-464-5085.

A simple assessment for families to use is the "Red Light, Yellow Light, Green Light" approach to drinking developed by Robert L. DuPont, M.D. An older adult in the green zone has no more than one drink in a twenty-four-hour period, and four drinks or less per week. The yellow zone is two to four drinks in twenty-four hours, and five to ten drinks per week. If an older adult can't stay in the green zone, there may be a drinking problem, and a professional assessment is needed.

Ⅲ

Ways Older Adults Misuse Medications

When drugs come from a doctor's prescription pad, misuse is harder to identify. We assume pharmaceutical drugs are only used for treating medical conditions, but many older adults take medications for nonmedical reasons.

Older adults misusing medications often believe they are following doctor's orders. They are *unintentional misusers*. The National Council on Patient Information and Education estimates that more than half of all prescription medications are used incorrectly. This leads to 125,000 deaths each year and $20 billion in health care costs.

Older adults unintentionally misuse medications for many reasons. They may misunderstand or not hear the doctor's directions. Doctors may prescribe the wrong medication or miscalculate the dose. Prescribed medications may be mixed with other drugs, causing undesirable interactions. Misuse occurs when older adults can't read labels. Arthritis prevents patients from opening medication bottles. A reluctance to ask for help contributes to drug misuse. Directions such as "Take the blue pills three times a day and the green pills once a day" lead to misuse because older people lose the ability to differentiate between the colors blue and green. Studies show that as many as three-quarters of older patients do not take their medications at the right time or in the correct amounts.

Although older patients with complicated medical protocol need more time with their doctors, consultations rarely exceed fifteen minutes. In that short time, doctors prescribe drugs patients may take for years. When older patients don't remember all the medications they're taking, doctors prescribe drugs without fully knowing if the drug is safe or necessary. This can lead to using more than one drug for the same problem, taking drugs that react adversely with one another, or using drugs for longer periods of time than is required or safe.

Doctors who are not trained in gerontology are at a disadvantage when managing the specific health care needs of aging patients. Twenty-three percent of older patients are given prescriptions for inappropriate medications. Some doctors overestimate the safety of medications, and some drug companies make inaccurate statements about their drugs. Lacking good information, doctors may prescribe medications safe for younger patients, but toxic to aging bodies. Some drugs are never safe for people over sixty-five years old. The *Journal of the American Medical Association (JAMA)* has published a list of twenty-three of these drugs:

Tranquilizers and Sleeping Aids
Diazepam (Valium): tranquilizer; addictive and too long acting
Chlordiazepoxide (Librium, Librax): tranquilizer; may cause falls
Flurazepam (Dalmane): sleeping aid; may cause falls
Meprobamate (Miltown, Deprol, Equagesic, Equanil): sleeping aid; may cause falls
Pentobarbital (Nebutal): sedative; addictive
Secobarbital (Seconal): sedative; addictive
Antidepressants
Amitriptyline (Elavil, Endep, Etrafon, Limbitrol, Triavil): often causes inability to urinate, dizziness, and drowsiness
Arthritis Drugs
Indomethacin (Indocin): can cause confusion and headaches
Phenylbutazone (Butazolidin): risk of bone marrow toxicity
Pain Relievers
Propoxyphene (Darvon Compound, Darvocet, Wygesic): addictive and little more effective than aspirin
Pentazocine (Talwin): addictive
Dementia Treatments
Cyclandelate: not shown to be effective
Isoxsuprine: not shown to be effective

Blood Thinners
Dipyridamole (Persantine): except for patients with artificial heart valves, not shown effective

Muscle Relaxants and Spasm Relievers
Cyclobenzaprine (Flexeril): can cause dizziness, drowsiness, and fainting
Orphenidrine (Norflex, Norgesic): can cause dizziness, drowsiness, and fainting
Methocarbamol (Robaxin): may cause dizziness or drowsiness
Carisoprodol (Soma): potential for central nervous system toxicity

Antinausea, Antivomiting Drugs
Trimethobenamide (Tigan): may cause drowsiness, dizziness, and other reactions

Antihypertensives
Propranolol (Inderal): feeling slowed mentally and physically
Methyldopa (Aldoril, Aldomet): feeling slowed mentally and physically
Reserpine (Regroton, Hydropres): depression

Diabetes Drugs
Chlorpropamide (Diabinese): can cause dangerous fluid retention

As people age, their bodies absorb, metabolize, distribute, and eliminate drugs differently than when they were younger. Normal adult doses of medications—both prescription and over-the-counter—can cause dangerous side effects and toxicity. By virtue of age, older patients may misuse medications without knowing it. This can happen in several ways:

- Most drugs are metabolized in the liver. As people age, their livers get smaller, blood flow decreases, liver enzyme levels decline, and, as a result, drugs metabolize slower and stay in the system longer. An older adult taking medications at normal adult doses can overdose.

- Similarly, some drugs are primarily excreted and metabolized by the kidneys. Many drugs are filtered out of the blood by the kidneys. With age, the kidneys shrink, blood flow decreases, and filtering slows down. Drugs not efficiently eliminated from the body stay active longer.

- Even when body weight stays the same, the percentage of body fat increases and lean mass decreases with age. Since some medications, such as sleeping aids and tranquilizers, are absorbed by fat cells, people with more body fat have higher concentrations of these drugs in their systems. Drugs absorbed by fat cells metabolize more slowly, staying in the body longer.

- The volume of water in the body decreases with age. With reduced water weight, some drugs become more potent. This is a bigger problem for older women who have less body water to begin with.

- In the bloodstream, drugs attach to proteins, one of which is albumin. Once attached, drug molecules are deactivated. Older adults have lower concentrations of albumin, so fewer drug molecules attach to proteins and more of the drug stays active in the body. The greater the number of unattached drug molecules, the greater chance that adult drug doses will reach toxic levels.

- Because age retards the functioning of the gastrointestinal tract, drugs stay in the stomach longer and move through the intestines slower. These delays impede the effects of drugs and can cause stomach and intestinal lesions.

- The capacity to tolerate a drug is different among the *young-old* (sixty-five to seventy-five), the *older-old* (seventy-five to eighty-five), and the *oldest-old* (eighty-five and older).

Some older adults intentionally abuse medications. Sleeping aids (sedatives/hypnotics), tranquilizers (anxiolytics), and pain pills (opiates) are common medications of abuse. Seeking pleasurable effects or attempting to ease feelings of grief and loneliness, older adults take larger doses than recommended. Over time, they build a tolerance to the drug. The same dose becomes ineffective because the nervous system has adapted. Achieving the same effect now requires larger amounts of the drug. Older adults go to several doctors for multiple prescriptions, or they combine medications with alcohol to boost the effect of the drug. Misuse may lead to staying on drugs like Valium and Librium (benzodiazepines) for years even though studies show that older adults shouldn't take these drugs for more than four weeks, and then taper off them.

Tranquilizers commonly prescribed for anxiety are Xanax, Librium, Valium, Ativan, Serax, and BuSpar. All these medications, except BuSpar, are benzodiazepines. They can cause residual sedation during waking hours and symptoms such as decreased attention, memory, cognitive function, and motor coordination. They are also attributed to increased falls and car accidents among the elderly. Some benzodiazepines are safer than others for older adults but should be used with extreme caution and only as a last option. All benzodiazepines have the potential for physiological dependence, even when taken at prescribed doses for as little as two months. Withdrawal symptoms include anxiety, agitation, nausea, loss of appetite, insomnia, dizziness, poor coordination, difficulty concentrating, depersonalization, confusion, and seizures. Older adults weaning themselves off benzodiazepines can mistake these withdrawal symptoms for the problem the medication was originally prescribed for and, consequently, begin taking the drug again.

The most common sleeping aids include several benzodiazepines: Dalmane, Centrax, Doral, Restoril, and Halcion. According to the National Institutes of Health, two out of three prescriptions for these drugs are written for older adults. Since long-term use of these drugs can cause a "rebound insomnia" and withdrawal, the National Institutes of Health cautions against the use of hypnotic benzodiazepines as the mainstay for treating insomnia. No studies show that these drugs are effective beyond thirty continuous nights. After that, the older adult may be using the drug only to stave off withdrawal symptoms—increased pulse rate, hand tremors, insomnia, nausea or vomiting, and anxiety.

Halcion has been reported as causing bizarre panic and delusional reactions, and adverse side effects such as confusion, agitation, anxiety, and blackouts. Antihistamines are also used as sleeping aids, but they can cause dependence within days, problems with balance, central nervous system depression, and confusion. Older adults living alone should avoid antihistamines.

The Center for Substance Abuse Treatment recommends that "symptomatic treatment of insomnia with medications be limited to seven to ten days with frequent monitoring and reevaluation if the prescribed drug will be used for more than two or three weeks. Intermittent dosing at the smallest possible dose is preferred, and no more than a thirty-day supply of hypnotics should be prescribed."

Pain pills are needed to manage severe pain resulting from surgery, accidents, and some illnesses. Most acute pain doesn't last more than hours or days, so the need for pain pills is short-term. Longer use of opiate pain medication can result in a physiological dependence, but this is managed by slowly withdrawing from the drug. The danger of addiction occurs when older adults misuse opiates or if they have a history of alcoholism. Withdrawal from opiates causes symptoms of restlessness, dysphoric mood, joint and muscle aches, nausea, vomiting, diarrhea, fever, and insomnia. Some of the commonly prescribed opiates are Tylenol #3, Robitussin AC, Vicoden, Lortab, Demerol, Percodan and Percocet, Darvon, and Talwin.

Misuse of medications, whether it's deliberate or inadvertent, leads to serious consequences. Addiction is one consequence of misuse. Other problems include extended illness, depression, toxic drug interactions, accidents, hospitalization, admission into nursing homes, cognitive impairment, and death. To avoid drug misuse, families need to partner with older adults, doctors, and pharmacists. Use an up-to-date reference guide to prescription and over-the-counter drugs to research medications. Determine if each drug is safe and necessary. An efficient way to do this is to participate in a "brown bag day." Dump all prescription and over-the-counter drugs in a bag and take them to a doctor or pharmacist for review. Repeat this once a year or every time a new medication is prescribed. When sedatives or tranquilizers are being prescribed for long-term use (over four weeks), ask the older adult and the doctor these questions:

- Is using the drug to solve the problem preventing the older adult's personal growth? Are there ways to alleviate the problem without medication, such as relaxation techniques, grief work, or counseling?
- Is using the drug preventing the older adult from discovering the source of the problem and taking healthy actions to deal with it appropriately?
- What nondrug recommendations did the doctor present to the patient before writing the prescription, or was the drug the first line of treatment? What are the nondrug alternatives?

For more information on safely using prescription drugs, contact The National Council on Patient Information and Education. Visit their Web site at www.talkaboutrx.org to get facts about medications and older adults, medicine record forms, a medication checkup kit, and to learn how to talk to an older person about medications. The site has a page in Spanish, and brochures are available in English, Spanish, and Asian languages. You can contact them at 301-656-8565.

Go to the resource section at the back of this book and take the quiz "Are Prescription and Over-the-Counter Drugs Used Safely?" Keep in mind that over-the-counter drugs can cause side effects, interact negatively with other medications, contain high levels of alcohol, cause drowsiness, and, in some cases, be addictive. The older adult's primary care physician should be informed of all drugs, supplements, herbal remedies, and vitamins the older adult is using.

⚓

Addiction to Prescription Drugs

Once use or misuse evolves into addiction, older adults become deceptive and secretive about their drug use. They are both ashamed and afraid of losing the drug. They become preoccupied with the drug. Much effort goes into protecting their supply while covering up the problem.

Addiction to prescription drugs is harder to detect than addiction to street drugs. We aren't surprised when someone using illegal drugs becomes addicted; we almost expect it. But we don't expect people using mood-altering prescription drugs to become addicted—especially our aging parents and grandparents. Getting drugs from a doctor appears legal, legitimate, and safe.

The older addicted patient is never exposed to the consequences of obtaining drugs from the street. For instance, pharmacy-bought drugs are much more affordable than street drugs. At the pharmacy, Percodan costs eighty-five cents per pill. On the street, it's seven dollars. Valium is a dollar a pill compared to six dollars on the street. Supporting a habit at the drugstore is more affordable than buying from a drug dealer; therefore, older adults have fewer financial problems associated with their addiction. And, although using prescription drugs nonmedically qualifies as an illegal use of controlled substances, this law is difficult to enforce. We've yet to hear of a grandmother arrested for obtaining tranquilizers from four different doctors.

When an older adult initially becomes addicted to mood-altering prescription drugs, several early symptoms emerge.

She'll begin taking the next dose of the drug earlier than scheduled. Needing more of the drug to get the same effect, she'll double or triple her dose. She begins to feel excited about taking the drug and looks forward to the "high," or feelings of euphoria. A few hours after taking the drug, she becomes lethargic. She experiences mood swings and insomnia. The drug is a central part of her life, but if she's questioned about her medications, she'll minimize how much she takes.

Dr. Robert L. DuPont, in his book *The Selfish Brain: Learning from Addiction,* identifies addiction in the following seven points:

1. Addiction means powerlessness over use of alcohol and other drugs.
2. Addiction both feeds on and causes self-centeredness, sensitivity to criticism, and dishonesty.
3. Addicts are not responsible for their disease, *but* they are responsible for what they do about their disease, at all stages of their disease.
4. Abstinence is necessary for recovery from addiction, *but* abstinence is not sufficient for recovery.
5. Getting well has a spiritual dimension that overcomes self-centeredness and dishonesty.
6. Recovery most often comes from participation in the lifelong fellowship of a Twelve Step program, such as Alcoholics Anonymous.
7. Addiction is a family disease—family members commonly suffer from codependence, and they are part of the progression of the disease. They usually need to participate in the process of recovery, using Al-Anon, Codependents Anonymous, Adult Children of Alcoholics, and other Twelve Step programs.

In order to maintain the status quo of addiction, older adults unconsciously use defense mechanisms to prevent others from interfering. Denial is the most common defense used by all addicted people, but when the drugs are prescribed by a doctor, denial is more resilient and tougher to break through.

Rationalizing, minimizing, and projecting sustain denial. An older adult uses rationalization to prove she doesn't have a drug problem. A classic line of rationalization is: "The doctor gives me these pills for pain. Without them, I couldn't live with the pain. Do you want me to suffer like that?" The fact that doctors can't find a cause for the pain is dismissed with, "Just because those doctors haven't found the problem yet doesn't mean I don't have pain." The older adult is creating reasons why using the drugs is legitimate.

Minimizing is an attempt to make the problem look insignificant. An older adult may say something like this: "You're making a big fuss over nothing, dear. My doctor knows exactly how many sleeping pills I take, and he says it's perfectly all right if I take an extra one when I really need it. Feeling a little drowsy once in a while is better than not sleeping at all." Minimizing is a way of making you believe your perceptions of the problem are exaggerated and faulty.

Projection is how an addicted older adult keeps the focus off himself by placing it onto others. Projection usually sounds like blame: "You're always complaining and nagging. It's a wonder I can continue to live with you. You're the one who needs serious help." When an addicted person uses projection, you quickly find you are defending yourself, and the point you were making about the drug use is lost in the shuffle.

When older adults rationalize, minimize, and project, they are also deceiving themselves. Abraham Twerski writes about this self-deception in his book *Addictive Thinking:* "Everyone gets taken in by addictive thinking, but the person *most* affected by it is the one who is doing the deceptive thinking, the addict.... Until denial is overcome, addicts are not lying when they say they aren't dependent on chemicals. They are truly unaware of their dependency."

Older adults addicted to prescription mood-altering drugs are rarely aware they have a problem. They believe they're using medications for legitimate, medical reasons. The self-deception and mind-altering effects of the drugs make it impossible for addicted people to observe their behaviors logically or rationally. They cannot see themselves as others see them.

Manipulation is another symptom of chemical dependency. To maintain an addiction, people learn how to manipulate others into helping them. They con doctors into giving them more drugs. They lie, deceive, and cover up. Addiction and honesty do not function simultaneously. As the addiction progresses, the older adult is forced to become increasingly dishonest in order to keep up with the demands of the addiction. He must convince doctors and relatives that the drug is for medical use rather than to feed an addiction. A chart published by Dr. DuPont in *New Jersey Medicine* differentiates between medical and nonmedical use:

Medical Use	Nonmedical Use
The intent is to treat a diagnosed illness	The intent is to alter mood
The effect is to make life better	The effect is to make life worse
The pattern of use is steady and sensible	The pattern of use is chaotic and high dose
The use of the medication is legal	The use of the medication is illegal
Control of use is shared with physician	Use is self-controlled

There are times when prescription drugs used for medical purposes cause physiological dependence. But this is different from addiction. For example, when a patient has been on Vicoden for several weeks to treat pain, he may develop a physical tolerance to the drug. If the drug is stopped abruptly, he'll go into withdrawal—with shakes, nausea, chills, cramps, mood swings, and anxiety. To avoid this, doctors gradually decrease the dose.

This type of physiological dependence is not the same as chemical dependency. Older adults physiologically dependent on a medication do not have a compulsion to use the drug. Nor do they have cravings or ongoing problems once the drug is discontinued. Dr. DuPont highlights the distinction between addiction and physiological dependence in *New Jersey Medicine:*

Characteristics of Physiological Dependence

- a cellular adaptation to presence of a substance
- withdrawal symptoms upon abrupt discontinuation
- not associated with relapse
- a benign, temporary problem
- common to many substances used in medicine including steroids, antidepressants, and antiepilepsy and antihypertensive medicines
- best treated by gradual dose reduction

Characteristics of Addiction

- loss of control
- continued use despite problems associated with use
- denial
- relapse
- a complex, behavioral, lifelong, malignant problem
- limited to chemically dependent people
- not a complication of medical treatment unless there is a prior history of chemical dependence
- best treated by specific chemical dependence treatment

A physiological dependence ends with successful detoxification, but addiction is a complex, progressive disease that causes ongoing negative consequences. If you're not sure whether your older relative is chemically dependent, turn to the back of this book and take the quiz "Signs of Alcoholism and Drug Abuse in Older People."

David M. Smith, M.D., of the American Society of Addiction Medicine, quoted in Rod Colvin's book *Prescription Drug Addiction: The Hidden Epidemic,* says: "When it comes to long-term abuse of prescription drugs, there's no question that there is a cumulative effect, and it can reduce life expectancy by about fifteen years. . . . We take prescription drug abuse too lightly as a health issue."

As widespread and serious as it is, addiction goes largely undetected by medical professionals and families. Families don't see the problem clearly because they suffer from their own denial. Even though addiction affects at least one out of ten older adults, it is the last thing families consider when an aging loved one is faltering. Alzheimer's disease is investigated before addiction. *A beloved grandmother or adored father can't be addicted to drugs.*

Most professionals prescribing and dispensing drugs—doctors and pharmacists—are poorly educated about addiction and are unlikely to diagnose the problem. A recent study by the National Center on Addiction and Substance Abuse at Columbia University found that 94 percent of primary care physicians missed the diagnosis of chemical dependency. More than half of the doctors surveyed said they do not ask about substance abuse. And, perhaps most startling, only 2 percent of the physicians said they believe drug rehabilitation is effective.

Families sometimes ignore a suspected addiction to prescription drugs out of a misguided sense of protecting the older adult's privacy. They allow the problem to continue, thinking the older adult and his doctor will handle the problem. But an older adult's denial combined with a doctor's lack of education can be a recipe for disaster. Families must educate themselves, partner with the medical professionals, consult with addiction specialists, and learn to properly intervene on addiction. If left untreated, prescription drug addiction diminishes the older adult's quality of life, robs him of his independence, leads to increased medical problems, creates growing burdens for caregivers, and results in early death.

⚓

Alcohol and the Older Woman

Most alcoholism research has focused on men, but recent studies show there are differences between men and women in their use of alcohol. Fewer women drink, but of those who drink heavily, the consequences can come faster and harder than among their male counterparts.

Most older adults with drinking problems are men who have had a long history of heavy drinking. Older women are less likely to drink than men. When they drink, they drink less. But more women than men experience late onset alcoholism. Alcohol's effect on women's health happens more quickly.

Older women become intoxicated faster from smaller amounts of alcohol. According to the National Institute on Alcohol Abuse and Alcoholism, this happens for two reasons. First, women have lower body water content than men of comparable size, and, as women age, their body water content declines. Alcohol diffuses throughout body water, so smaller quantities of body water cause higher concentrations of alcohol in women's blood than in the bood of men drinking the same amount of alcohol. Blood alcohol concentration in women is comparable to pouring the same quantity of alcohol into a small bucket of water versus a large bucket.

Second, women have smaller amounts of the enzyme responsible for metabolizing alcohol in the stomach. This contributes to differences in blood alcohol concentrations between men and women, and women's heightened vulnerability to alcohol-related health consequences. Studies show that alcoholic women have virtually none of these enzymes in their stomachs. When they drink, alcohol goes straight into their bloodstream.

Alcohol is more damaging to a woman's liver than a man's. Women develop liver disease, such as cirrhosis, in a much shorter time than men do and after drinking less. A recent study by Columbia University found that women who have as few as two drinks a day face significant risk of liver damage, whereas men have a similar risk at six drinks a day. Women can increase their risk for breast cancer if they drink as little as one ounce of alcohol a day. The risk increases as drinking increases.

Women are more susceptible to the risks of alcohol than men in the following ways:

- Women become intoxicated quicker.
- Women become addicted sooner.
- Women's health problems are more serious.
- Women have increased risk for heart disease, ulcers, osteoporosis, pancreatitis, and memory loss.
- Alcohol affects the liver more severely and in a shorter period of time.
- More women die of cirrhosis, proportionately, than men.
- Women experience increased toxic effects of alcohol on the heart muscle.
- Women develop chronic pancreatitis with shorter drinking histories.
- Women are twice as likely to die from alcohol-related diseases.
- Women develop hypertension, anemia, and malnutrition more quickly than men.
- More women develop drinking problems later in life than men.
- Women are less likely to be diagnosed for alcoholism or receive alcoholism treatment.

These differences between men and women may be related to women's lower body water content, body weight, and stomach enzymes. Combined with advanced age, these factors cause greater harm.

NIAAA reports that drinking behavior in women differs with age, marital status, and life roles. Older women report a lower use of alcohol than women under thirty-four. Alcohol dependence is most prevalent among middle-aged women. Women of all ages tend to pattern their drinking habits after the drinking behavior of spouses, siblings, and close friends. Women are more susceptible to peer pressure. This could be one reason why some women, living in retirement communities with numerous drinking activities, begin drinking more heavily in later life.

Widowed, divorced, and unmarried women are more likely to have drinking problems than married women. Studies focusing on the drinking behavior of female twins show that marital status influences the genetic predisposition to alcoholism. Marriage is an environmental modifier—married women tend to drink less and, therefore, have a lower risk for developing alcoholism.

Other studies show that women who have multiple life roles have fewer alcohol-related problems than women who have only one life role. Surprising to some, women who are wives, mothers, and workers outside the home have fewer drinking problems. When a woman loses her roles, she is more likely to abuse alcohol. For an older woman, this can be the "empty nest syndrome" or the death of her husband. Losses and changes can lead to a lack of meaning and connection to life; but life can become a nightmare when self-medicating with alcohol turns into addiction.

Marty Mann, a New York socialite and the first woman to get sober in Alcoholics Anonymous, describes the pain brought on by her alcoholism:

I was in complete darkness as to what it was that was happening to me, and I spent five years trying to find out. Alcoholism is a progressive illness. During those five years I rode the chute-to-chute to hell. It was no fun. . . . And I suffered all the torments, although all this was while I was seeking help. I was desperately trying to find out what was wrong—what, if anything, could be done. No one could tell me. And no one could help me. I thought I had a severe mental illness. . . . I was going headlong toward death and destruction (from *Mrs. Marty Mann: The First Lady of Alcoholics Anonymous,* by Sally Brown and David R. Brown).

⚓

How to Help an Addicted Older Adult

A Self-preserving Disease

Alcoholism is a disease that keeps itself secret from the victim. While the disease is dismantling the alcoholic's life, the alcoholic is working to preserve the disease. We can compare an alcoholic to someone who thinks throwing gasoline on a burning house makes sense. Faced with the inferno caused by addiction, alcoholics always return to the same thought: *Another drink is the solution.* This delusional thinking is not self-induced; it's a symptom of the disease.

Many people have tried to explain the workings of a mind controlled by alcoholism. Katherine Ketcham and William Asbury write in *Beyond the Influence:*

> Alcoholics in denial have been called stupid, stubborn, selfish, and pigheaded ... but in reality they are simply following the dictates of their addicted brains. This is why they can't accurately judge what's happening to them, why they stubbornly refuse to look at reality, and why they can't "just say no." Their brains are urging them on, using all sorts of physical and emotional prods. "Go ahead and take a drink, it won't hurt you," the brain cajoles.

Robert L. DuPont, M.D., in his book *The Selfish Brain: Learning from Addiction,* compares addiction to alcohol or other drugs to being hypnotized. He explains that the chemically dependent have no idea why they behave as they do. When asked, they simply make up reasons and excuses to explain the unexplainable. Dr. DuPont says:

> It is remarkable to see the ability of addiction to overcome even the most moral and sensible person. I have seen many physicians, teachers, ministers, and others of high intelligence and great moral strength turned into dishonest and irresponsible people by their addictions. But they and those who know them well are amazed by this, because they underestimate the power of addiction to control human behavior, regardless of intelligence or character.

The basic text *Alcoholics Anonymous,* commonly called the Big Book, describes delusional thinking of alcoholics: "Men and women drink essentially because they like the effect produced by alcohol. The sensation is so elusive that, while they admit it is injurious, they cannot after a time differentiate the true from the false. To them their alcoholic life seems the only normal one."

Gerald G. May, M.D., in his book *Addiction and Grace,* says: "One of the most significant hallmarks of addiction is the exquisite inventiveness that the mind can demonstrate in order to perpetuate addictive behaviors. Here, where the will fights against itself in a morass of mixed motivations and contradictory desires, the creative power of the brain is used unconsciously to subvert each and every attempt to control the addictive behavior."

In his book *Terry: My Daughter's Life-and-Death Struggle with Alcoholism,* former senator George McGovern describes Terry's inability to answer the question *why?* He writes: "An orderly went into the examination room to check on her. He found her curled up in a ball under a blanket, soaking wet, shivering and frightened. It was not the first time he had encountered Terry at St. Mary's. Dropping to his knees he asked: 'Why are you doing this to yourself?' Rocking in agony, she could only say, 'I don't know. I don't know.' And, indeed, she could never explain her cruel and punishing, self-inflicted bouts with alcohol." Elsewhere in the book, Senator McGovern quotes from Terry's personal diary: "How could I want to keep company with the same agent that has snatched from my grasp all that I have loved."

For alcoholics, alcohol is the way to normal. It's not entertainment, exhilaration, celebration, excitation, inspiration, or relaxation. It isn't a cover-up for past wounds or present-day worries. It's a required part of life, like breathing. Robert, a retired schoolteacher, describes it this way: "Do you remember back when you were a kid and you were swimming in a lake with your pals? Invariably, some kid would get the smart idea that it would be funny to dunk you under and not let you up. The joke was cute for only five or ten seconds when you were the fella' under the water. When you couldn't get back to the surface, things got serious. You'd fight, kick, scratch—anything to get a breath of air. That's how I felt when someone threatened my drinking."

Understanding that alcoholics aren't able to see drinking as a problem helps explain why we don't get far when we express our concerns. While we're identifying alcohol as the *problem,* the alcoholic sees it as the *solution.*

In the book *Love First: A New Approach to Intervention for Alcoholism and Drug Addiction,* Jeff Jay and Debra Jay explain: "You probably don't realize that you and the alcoholic are speaking two different languages. To you, alcohol is the obvious problem and sobriety is the logical solution. If the alcoholic would listen, you know he would put the bottle down forever. Of course, it rarely works that way. To the alcoholic, alcohol is not the problem; it's the solution. The problem is anybody or anything that gets in the way of his consumption of alcohol. You're talking about alcohol as the problem; he's talking about you as the problem. See the problem?"

⚓

Different Worldviews

The worldview of our elders is reflected in their maxims: Don't air your dirty laundry. Pick yourself up by your bootstraps. Put your best foot forward. Buck up. Actions speak louder than words. Make the best of it. Look on the bright side. Don't go looking for trouble. If you have nothing good to say, say nothing at all. Take the good with the bad. Leave well enough alone. Idle hands are the devil's workshop. Hold your tongue. Put on a happy face. Take it on the chin. Who do you think you are?

These maxims reflect thinking from a time before psycho-therapy or the self-help movement was part of the American consciousness, and they compound resistance to treatment. In *Another Country: Navigating the Emotional Terrain of Our Elders,* Mary Pipher explains what older people think of therapy: "Not only does this age group have no experience with the 'talking cure,' they have training in just the opposite. They learned to whisper words like *cancer* and *divorce*. They were taught that even to speak about an event made it more real. Thus, one way to protect oneself from painful events was not to talk about them, to pretend they didn't exist. Psychotherapy flies in the face of this theory."

How we experience our world is largely a factor of when we were born. People born in the first half of the 1900s see the world differently than those born in the second half. Older adults think and speak differently than their children and grandchildren. Older adults were raised to value hard work, a solid reputation, personal achievement, and self-sacrifice. Life isn't about feeling good; it's about doing good. Complaining gets you nowhere. If you stumble and fall, you're expected to get up, dust yourself off, and never look back. While younger generations spend time processing their feelings and working on issues, the older ones find it more sensible to pull weeds in the garden and get the ironing done. "Nothing a little hard work can't put right," they might say. Talking about their problems in a treatment setting is in direct opposition to the way they handle life's problems. Among younger generations, therapy is not only an accepted method of self-care, but also a symbol of sophistication and status. Older adults believe therapy is a mark of personal defeat.

Before you attempt to help an older adult, take the time to consider his worldview. Pay attention to the assumptions behind your words. You may think you are communicating a positive message, but the older adult may be hearing a threat. You say:

"I'm worried about your drinking. I think you need to get help for alcoholism." Your elder responds defensively: "What are you talking about? I'm not an alcoholic. How dare you suggest such a thing? You talk to me like I'm a bum." To the older adult, the word *alcoholic* is synonymous with *wino* or *town drunk.* Deborah Tannen, author of *I Only Say This Because I Love You,* explains, "Precisely because we can't really see the world from someone else's point of view, it is critical that we find ways to talk to each other so we can explain our points of view and work out solutions."

Taking into account that normal family life is commonly fraught with miscommunication between generations, how difficult is it to make yourself understood when you are also facing the denial and delusional thinking of alcoholism? Success with older adults requires sensitivity to the language of their generation.

⚏

Start with a Talk

Families talk about the alcohol or drug problem with everybody but the alcoholic. If you've never had a constructive, honest conversation with your older relative, it's a good place to begin. Of course, we can't talk about chemical dependency the same way we'd talk about the house needing a coat of paint or the car needing a tune-up. The problem is obvious to us, but it isn't to the older adult. We may show up as friend, but they see us as foe. We are at a distinct disadvantage before we open our mouths.

Talking one-on-one with a chemically dependent person is a difficult proposition. You may begin with high hopes but soon find yourself outmaneuvered. Your logic and rational arguments are easily bent and twisted by the alcoholic. Older adults who've been straight shooters their entire lives are transformed into skilled manipulators by their addiction. They'll easily dash your best-laid plans, and you'll walk away trying to figure out how things got turned around so quickly.

Set realistic expectations for your talk. Ask yourself, "What do I hope to achieve?" You may want the older adult to accept help immediately, but prepare yourself for denial, minimizing, and rationalizing. Unrealistic expectations can tempt you to give up on the older adult prematurely. Family members often end talks with older alcoholics by throwing their hands in the air and saying, "See? Nothing works. You can't get through to him." Don't fall into this trap. Adjust your expectations. It's realistic to assume that talking to the older adult will be your first step, not your last.

Plan your talk for a time when the older adult will most likely be sober. You cannot have a productive discussion with someone under the influence of mind-altering substances, because their brain is reacting to the effect of the drug, not to what you are saying. To an inebriated brain, nothing you say matters. The meaning of your words doesn't fully register. The impaired brain deciphers your words as little more than the obnoxious buzzing of insects about the alcoholic's head, and everything the alcoholic says is an attempt to swat you away. You may believe you and the alcoholic are having a heart-to-heart conversation, but an intoxicated older adult is incapable of the emotional intimacy such a conversation requires.

If your older relative is rarely sober or begins drinking early in the day, select a time when he or she is the most coherent. Mornings are usually best, or times when the older adult is known to abstain—before church, for instance. When mood-altering prescription medications are the problem, it is harder to determine when the older adult is sober. Use your own experiences and gather information from other family members to determine the best times to meet. When you arrive for your visit, if it becomes clear that the older adult is inebriated, postpone your talk.

Plan to meet with the older adult at a time free of distractions. Don't have a talk when children or other people uninvolved in the conversation are present. Allow yourself plenty of time. Don't begin a discussion fifteen minutes before the older adult is leaving for an appointment or when the telephone repairman is expected. Talk in a private place, not in a restaurant or other public setting. Select a place other than the older adult's home when possible, because an alcoholic has the advantage on his home turf. Of course, sometimes the alcoholic won't leave his home, and you have no choice but to go there.

Don't give the older adult advance notice that you want to talk about his drinking or other drug problems. If you say, "I'd like to set up a time when we can get together to talk about your addiction to tranquilizers," you'll thwart your best attempts to help by alerting the older adult's defense mechanisms. It is far better to keep your invitation for a get-together generic: "Are you free Saturday morning? Why don't we get together for coffee at my house?" If you live miles apart, you might say, "Mom, we haven't had a visit in such a long time, why don't you come here for a weekend?"

Ask another concerned family member or friend to join you in your talk with the older adult. Convincing an alcoholic to accept help is a formidable task, and, by including another person, you have a better chance. Select someone the alcoholic likes and respects: a lifelong friend, sibling, adult grandchild, or clergyperson. Whomever you choose, share this book with them as you prepare to discuss your concerns with the older alcoholic.

To avoid a communication breakdown, speak to the older adult's beliefs rather than from your beliefs. For instance, older adults often object to accepting help by saying: "I can't go in for treatment. What will people think?" Younger people usually counter this objection by saying: "Don't worry about what other people think. Do this for yourself." This response comes from the belief that we should do what's good for ourselves regardless of what others think about us. But this belief doesn't resonate with the worldview of aging people who value conformity and "fitting in" above independence and autonomy. An answer more sensitive to the older adult's way of thinking is: "Mother, if I've noticed that you've forgotten telephone conversations, I imagine I'm not the only person who realizes you don't remember. Your neighbor who found you disoriented after you'd been drinking knows something is wrong. The alcohol is damaging your reputation. I know you don't want that. Getting help will preserve your good standing in the community. Nobody needs to know you're in treatment unless you want them to know." This response acknowledges that the opinion of others is important to older adults while simultaneously presenting treatment as a tool to help preserve the older adult's good reputation.

Avoid words that increase the older adult's feelings of shame. *Alcoholic* and *drug addict* are words heavy with stigma. *Drunk* is a humiliating way to describe intoxication. Phrases such as *what are you doing to yourself?* and *why can't you stop?* imply blame. Using these words and phrases stirs up shame and triggers defense mechanisms. To keep defenses down, refer to the older adult's addiction as chemical dependency, alcohol dependence, or a medication problem. Use statements such as "how alcohol has turned on you" and "it's not your fault that you have this disease." Keep it in the forefront of your mind that you are talking about a disease, not a moral failing.

Be gentle and approach the older adult with love. Start by telling your aging relative how much you value them. You might say: "Dad, you've always been my Rock of Gibraltar. Throughout my life, I've known I could depend on you whenever I needed help. I can't thank you enough. Now I'm here for you because I love you, and I'm concerned for your health." Throughout your

discussion, maintain your tone of love and concern. Do not resort to blame, judgment, or anger. If the older adult gets angry,
this is not an excuse for you to become angry. In the past, you
may have reacted to the alcoholic's moods, but reaction isn't action. To get results, take action and avoid reacting.

When discussing the alcohol or medication problem with
the older adult, avoid talking about the distant past. Use recent
examples. As a rule of thumb, stay within the last six to twelve
months. Tap into issues the older adult cares about most. For
instance, older adults worry about developing dementia, losing
their health, and relinquishing independent living. If alcohol is
causing problems in any of these areas, these examples are
likely to gain the older adult's attention.

Don't recite a laundry list of every problem alcohol has
caused in the older adult's life. No matter how loving you sound,
an endless dirge of examples will humiliate the older adult.
When you choose your examples, strike a balance. Be honest
and clear, but preserve the alcoholic's dignity. If you don't, you
risk sounding abusive. Limit yourself to two or three examples.
Talk about what you have witnessed with your own eyes.
Hearsay sounds like gossip and will anger the older adult. Use
I-statements such as "I've noticed that alcohol has begun affecting your memory" or "I'm concerned because I see alcohol
threatening your safety and health." Sentences beginning with
the word you sound accusatory and should be avoided. Be brief,
but specific. Use dates and times, details of behaviors, and
amounts of alcohol or other drugs consumed. Older adults
can't see themselves clearly. Seeing themselves through your
eyes can open their eyes to how addiction is affecting them.

Pay attention to your tone and body language. You can say
all the right words, but what you are not saying can sometimes
speak louder. Body language includes facial expressions; hand,
arm, foot, leg, and body positions; and posture. For instance,
leaning forward and maintaining eye contact when the older

adult is talking to you indicates you are listening with interest. Looking away and fidgeting give the impression of impatient disinterest. Keep the silent language of your body consistent with your words and intentions.

If the alcoholic is not open to talking about her alcohol problem, don't force the issue. Take the longer view and remind yourself that this talk is your first step, not your last. You'll have a greater impact on the older adult if you respond to her reluctance by staying calm and saying: "I broached this topic with you today because I've been aware for some time that alcohol is causing serious problems in your life. As hard as this is for me, I know that talking with you directly about my concerns is the right thing to do. I want you to know I am here to help you overcome this problem. You may not want to talk about it today, but at least you know you can call me anytime, and I'll be ready to help."

On the other hand, if the older adult agrees to get help, be prepared to take immediate action. Have the number of a treatment center and the name of a person who schedules assessments in your pocket. Help the older adult take the first step by saying: "I took the time to find an excellent center. I was told we could give them a call today, and they would schedule a time for an assessment. Let's give them a call right now." If you wait to take action, you give the alcoholic a chance to change her mind.

⚓

A Conversation with an Addicted Older Adult

Tom was a late onset alcoholic. His problems with drinking started in his sixties, but worsened in his early seventies, after his wife died. One night, after drinking several glasses of Scotch, Tom walked away from chicken frying on the stovetop and passed out on the living-room couch. The burning chicken set off the fire alarm. When the fire department arrived, the house was filled with smoke, the chicken was charred, and Tom was asleep on the couch. He was rushed to the hospital and treated for smoke inhalation.

The next day, Tom's daughter Laurie scolded him. She told him he'd almost killed himself, and he needed to get control over his drinking. Tom agreed with his daughter. He said: "I don't know how I let myself drink that much Scotch. I must have forgotten how much I'd had earlier. I can promise you it'll never happen again."

Two months later, Laurie got a call from the police. Tom was found walking through his neighborhood disoriented. The officer said he could smell liquor on his breath. The police brought Tom home. Laurie rushed over to her dad's house. Intoxicated, Tom began sobbing. He talked about being lonely and feeling old and useless. Laurie, overwhelmed by her dad's tears, comforted him and said: "I know you've had it hard since Mom died, but you can't keep drinking so much. Maybe you'd feel like your old self if you did some volunteer work at the hospital." Tom agreed that volunteering was a good solution.

Three weeks later, Laurie got a call from Tom's neighbor. The neighbor said she hadn't seen Tom for a couple of days, his mail and newspapers weren't picked up, and he wasn't answering the phone. When Laurie arrived at Tom's house, she found him drunk and watching television with all the shades drawn. Empty Scotch bottles were scattered around the room. Laurie angrily asked her dad why he was drunk in the middle of the day. Hadn't he promised to cut down on the drinking? Tom responded with his own anger, telling his daughter he didn't need her interfering in his life.

This is a typical family response to a chemically dependent older adult. The addiction goes unnoticed or ignored until a crisis hits. Then family members react to the crisis without preparation or guidance. In this example, Laurie made two classic mistakes when talking with her father. First, she reacted to what

Tom told her rather than evaluating what he did. By doing so, she was manipulated by Tom's words—*I can do it on my own; I'm lonely and useless; don't interfere*—and ignored the seriousness of what was happening to her father.

Second, Laurie presented her father with vague, unworkable solutions for his problem: *You need to get control over your drinking* was her first suggestion. If alcoholics could control their drinking, they wouldn't be alcoholic. *Volunteer at the hospital* was her second suggestion. Improving the life of a chemically dependent person does not cure addiction. It works the other way around. Recovery from addiction is a requirement for an improved life. Finally, Laurie used anger as a response to Tom's intoxication. Her anger triggered his anger, and he alienated Laurie by telling her to stop interfering in his life. Laurie is left feeling rejected, frustrated, angry, and ready to give up. All three drinking crises could have served as opportunities for interventions on Tom's alcoholism, but Laurie didn't know how to talk to her dad in a language he could understand.

Let's rewind and see how this story unfolds once Laurie is trained to talk to her dad and handle crisis differently. After the incident with the stovetop fire, Laurie arrives at the hospital. She learns that her father is intoxicated. Laurie asks the doctor to test her father's blood alcohol concentration (BAC). The next day, while Tom is still in the hospital, Laurie and the doctor talk to Tom. They tell him he had a BAC of .18 when admitted into the hospital. The doctor explains that this indicates an alcohol problem. The doctor recommends that Tom go to a local treatment center for an assessment. Tom insists this was a onetime problem, and he will never let it happen again. Laurie gently and lovingly says: "Dad, this is a problem I've seen get worse over the last couple of years. It's not your fault. The doctor can tell you it is a medical problem and not uncommon among people as they get older. Alcohol has a greater effect on an aging body." Tom continues to insist he can handle the problem

on his own, steadfastly refusing to get a professional assessment. The doctor tells Tom he could experience dangerous
alcohol withdrawal if he stops drinking without medical assistance. Still Tom refuses. Laurie responds by making an agreement with Tom: "Dad, I'm not the only one who is concerned.
Sue and Paul are worried about you, too. Make a promise to all
of us that if you cannot stop drinking on your own, you will do it
our way and go for treatment. Will you give me your solemn
word?" Tom, glad to be off the hook, readily agrees.

Two months later, Laurie gets a call from the police, who
have found Tom intoxicated and disoriented. Laurie immediately drives to her dad's home, but waits until the next day when
he is sober to talk to him. Laurie is joined by her sister and
brother, Sue and Paul. They sit down to talk with their father,
calmly explaining what happened the night before. Tom doesn't
remember, so they show him a copy of the police report. Laurie
says: "Dad, you've given this your best effort. If anyone could
beat this problem on their own, it would be you. This is not your
fault, but, since things haven't worked out as you had hoped, it's
time to get help. I spoke with your doctor, and he stressed that
you have a disease requiring professional treatment. We've
found a beautiful center that helps many fine people in your
age group overcome problems caused by alcohol dependence.
Sue, Paul, and I love you and have arranged for your admission
this afternoon, as we agreed we would. I'll help pack your bag,
and then we'll all go together."

Can you see how Laurie's new approach put her in a much
better position for successfully motivating her father to accept
help? She didn't focus on what Tom *said*, but on what he *did*.
When Tom was unable to control his drinking on his own,
Laurie returned to the agreement Tom made in the hospital
with her and the doctor. Laurie included her brother and sister
in the meeting, uniting the family in a show of support for treatment. Laurie focused on positive action—accepting treatment

at an alcohol rehabilitation center for older adults—rather than vague solutions. Tom may still refuse treatment, but if he does, Laurie knows she's done the right thing and is well situated to help Tom in the future.

Most families attempt to help the older adult in the same way Laurie did initially. But previous mistakes don't block future success. Change the way you talk to your older adult, and he will begin changing the way he responds to you.

⚏

Involving the Family Physician

When families ask what they should do about an addiction problem, they are usually referred to their family doctor. However, most doctors, including psychiatrists, have little or no training in addictions and know very little about diagnosing and treating the disease. But with some planning on your part, a doctor can be a powerful ally in motivating your older relative to accept treatment. First, however, you need to understand the limitations of medical doctors who are not trained in addiction medicine.

For the most part, physicians' attitudes about alcoholism reflect those of society at large. Doctors who lack particular training in alcoholism commonly view alcoholics as weak-willed people who don't have the moral rectitude to use alcohol in a responsible manner. Some doctors refer to alcoholism as a "lifestyle choice." This erroneous thinking can be compared to the past, when mental illness was considered a choice, and people who "chose" mental illness were guilty of a criminal offense.

Many doctors fear offending their aging patients with questions about their drinking habits. Most doctors also admit they don't ask these questions because they expect patients will only lie about alcohol or other drug problems. Joseph Califano, president of the National Center on Addiction and Substance Abuse, speaking about doctors' abilities to treat addiction, states that doctors are uncomfortable talking to patients about addiction and drug abuse and would rather avoid the topic.

According to a study published in the *Journal on Trauma,* doctors are discouraged from discussing substance abuse because of the legal rights of insurance companies to deny coverage for injuries related to alcohol or other drugs. Impairment due to alcohol consumption is a leading factor in falls and hip fractures among the elderly; however, physicians may not assess older adults' blood alcohol content at the time of the injury, fearing insurance companies will deny the claim. These concerns are based on laws that exist in most states and allow insurance carriers to deny payment to patients who are impaired by alcohol at the time of injury. These laws increase the probability that alcoholism will go undiagnosed and untreated, resulting in future incidents of accidents and other illnesses. Dr. Frederick Rivara, director of the Harborview Prevention and Research Center, and principal researcher in the study, says, "Failing to pay attention to alcohol abuse in a trauma patient could be viewed as being as negligent as failing to diagnose and treat hypertension in a middle-aged man with heart problems."

Statistics indicate that physicians have a tendency to overprescribe medications to older adults and prescribe more mood-altering drugs to women than men. A 1998 study by the National Center on Addiction and Substance Abuse at Columbia University reviewed mood-altering medications prescribed to 13,000 older women over a period of six months. The report found that half of the prescriptions for tranquilizers and sleeping pills were either unnecessary or should have been prescribed for shorter periods of time. One in four women is prescribed a psychoactive prescription drug, according to the study. The research also shows that doctors don't recognize symptoms of substance abuse in older female patients. When primary care physicians were presented with common signs of alcohol abuse, only 1 percent of the doctors correctly diagnosed the problem as substance abuse. Eighty percent diagnosed the problem as depression. These findings help explain why so many older alcoholics are prescribed antidepressants while their alcoholism goes untreated.

In addition to being insufficiently trained in the field of addictions, some doctors are themselves heavy drinkers or alcoholics. Research shows that one in ten doctors is a daily drinker. Studies conducted at several medical schools found that 20 percent or more of medical students working in residency programs showed signs of alcoholism. Although most doctors do not abuse substances, those who do are less likely to regard their patients' drinking or drug problems as abnormal.

The federal government has responded to the lack of education on chemical dependency among doctors and other health care professionals by forming the Interdisciplinary Faculty Development Program to Improve Substance Abuse Education. This program will train faculty in medical schools to teach students to recognize substance abuse in their patients. Most doctors haven't had the benefit of this type of training. To bolster your chances of a good outcome with a physician, find a doctor who is certified in addiction medicine by the American Society of Addiction Medicine.

To alert the older adult's primary care physician, call or write a letter documenting the symptoms of the older adult's chemical dependency. Doctors have very little time, so your telephone call or letter should be precise and short. Ask the doctor if he or she is experienced in substance abuse assessment. If not, fax the doctor a copy of the resources listed below. In a later chapter in this section, we'll show how a letter written by the older adult's doctor can be used during a family intervention.

To find a doctor certified in addiction medicine, contact the American Society of Addiction Medicine by calling 301-656-3920 and ask for the membership assistant. To request a referral by e-mail, visit its Web site at www.asam.org. Ask for a referral to a gerontologist with a specialty in addictions in the older adult's home area. If the older adult refuses to see a new doctor, ask the primary care physician to consult with the specialist.

The following resources, produced specifically for doctors, are excellent education tools about older adults and chemical dependency:

- A twelve-page guide published by the National Institute on Alcohol Abuse and Alcoholism, *The Physician's Guide to Helping Patients with Alcohol Problems,* can be downloaded by logging onto www.niaaa.nih.gov/publications/physicn.htm. Or call 301-443-3860 and ask for publication number 95-3769. NIAAA will send a copy at no charge.
- The U.S. Department of Health and Human Services publishes a desk reference for doctors titled *Substance Abuse among Older Adults: Physicians Guide.* It provides targeted information pertinent to medical doctors and is available at no cost by contacting the National Clearinghouse for Alcohol and Drug Information toll free at 800-729-6686 or 301-468-2600; TDD (for the hearing impaired) 800-487-4889.
- The American Medical Association, in the report *Alcoholism in the Elderly: Diagnosis, Treatment, Prevention,* publishes guidelines for primary care physicians. The seventeen-page report is free to doctors by writing to the Department of Geriatric Health, American Medical Association, 515 North State Street, Chicago, IL 60610, or call 312-464-5085.
- Max A. Schneider, M.D., has created a video to increase awareness among doctors and other elder-care providers who often overlook substance abuse as the root cause of older adults' health problems. The twenty-eight-minute video, titled *Looking Forward to Tomorrow: Medical Aspects of Seniors and Substances,* addresses issues regarding the use

of alcohol, prescription medications, and over-the-counter medications, and how to maximize the future health of seniors. The price of the video is $29.95, and it can be ordered by calling 714-639-0062.

ⅲ

Take Advantage of a Crisis

An alcoholic's crisis is a family's opportunity. When a crisis occurs, it weakens the alcoholic's internal defense mechanisms. Feeling regret for her behavior, the alcoholic may even admit that alcohol or other drugs are causing some problems. Since alcoholics don't reach out for help when their lives are running smoothly, it's best to reach out to them when a crisis begins chipping away at their denial system. Families who harness a crisis and use it properly have a good chance of motivating the older adult to accept treatment.

Alcoholics believe their own defense mechanisms. Alcoholics sustain a rosy image of their alcohol use even as addiction extracts an ever-greater toll. Remembering alcohol or other drug use as pleasurable in spite of its negative consequences is called euphoric recall. Dr. Vernon Johnson, in his book *I'll Quit Tomorrow*, describes this phenomenon:

> In every one of these excessive drinking episodes, the alcoholic will be, the next day, only able to recall euphorically. That is, the chemical alcohol so affects the brain that in no way can alcoholics remember the slurred words, or weaving gait, or exaggerated gesticulations, or broken sentences. The recollection is, "I was a terrific hit. Everybody loved me and I did just fine." For alcoholics, this area of perception and memory distortion contributes powerfully to the inability to see and appreciate reality, and to the failure to recognize and accept the fact that they're in a downward spiral.

Crisis pulls back the veil of euphoric recall. The alcoholic sees a glimpse of the alcohol or other drug problem. Defense mechanisms begin breaking down. The alcoholic has a moment of clarity, and this briefly opens the door to family and friends who want to step in and help. But few know how to take advantage of this short-lived opportunity.

Most families react by *removing* the crisis rather than *using* the crisis. If Grandpa's driving while under the influence, relatives find a way he can get around town without letting him drive himself. Family members take turns chauffeuring him from place to place, or they hire a transportation service. They don't focus on Grandpa's alcoholism; they focus on his drunk driving. Their solution isn't finding a way to treat the disease, but on preventing arrests or accidents. The family, relieved that they've solved another problem, is unaware they've made it easier for the alcoholic to stay sick. Due to their efforts, Grandpa's drinking is no longer a block to his independence (that is, his access to transportation), so now he drinks with impunity.

Each time families remove a crisis, they make way for the next crisis. As the disease progresses, crises arrive closer together and with more magnitude. Families who rush to solve each new crisis in the alcoholic's life dwell in perpetual crisis. To break the cycle, stop treating crisis as an enemy. Instead, look at crisis as a friend opening a door to opportunity. As author Richard Bach reminds us: "There is no such thing as a problem without a gift for you in its hands." Learn to see the gift each crisis brings you. A loving family intervention paired with a crisis is a powerful tool. Many older adults are relieved when their families help them do what they cannot do for themselves—ask for help.

Not all crises need to be major in the life of the older adult. Crises come in different sizes. Some are big, and others are small. But one can be as effective as the other. Being told her granddaughter is afraid to visit her because "Granny scares me when she acts and talks funny" can be as devastating to an older adult as a diagnosis of cirrhosis. When a crisis attacks something near and dear to the older adult, it's a good time to intervene.

Prepare yourself *before* a crisis occurs. Learn how to use a crisis effectively. Planning a family intervention requires time. If the crisis subsides before you take action, the older adult is less pliable than when the crisis is a burning issue. It's been said that the definition of luck is "when preparation meets opportunity." Preparation allows you to take advantage of opportunities—or crises—as soon as they arise.

⚞

Join Hands

There is strength in numbers. Nowhere is this truer than when a family is facing the addiction of a loved one. Use your numbers; build a team. Reach out to other people who are concerned about the well-being of the older adult. Ask them if they will join hands and learn a way to motivate the alcoholic to accept help. Taking this step, you put in motion changes that can alter the direction of your family's future. As writer and physician Oliver Wendell Holmes wrote, "I find the great thing in this world is not so much where we stand as in what direction we are moving."

The power of a team can trump the power of addiction. Triumphing over addiction always involves groups. Treatment centers use clinical *teams* and *group* counseling to treat alcoholism. Following treatment, alcoholics are referred to aftercare *groups*. Alcoholics Anonymous is based on the power of the *group*. The first word of the Twelve Steps of Alcoholics Anonymous is *we*. While our individual efforts are routinely subverted by the insidious nature of addiction, groups pose a formidable foe to the disease.

Begin building a team by making a list of each person important in the older adult's life. Don't edit anyone off your list just yet. You'll select your final team after reviewing all the names. First, write the names of immediate family members and other close relatives. Next, write the names of the older adult's dearest friends. Then add other significant people, such as the older adult's doctor, pastor or rabbi, caregiver, family lawyer, and others who have a trusted professional relationship with the older adult. Your goal is to select three to eight names from this list to make up your team.

When you've completed your list, cross off anyone who is a practicing alcoholic or addict. Team members don't have to be teetotalers, but people who are *actively* alcoholic can sabotage a family intervention or turn against team members. Practicing alcoholic team members rationalize, minimize, or deny the older adult's problem. Talking openly about the older adult's addiction is a threat to his or her own defense system.

Don't exclude people from your team because they live too far away or they lead busy lives. Most people are willing to go to any length to help the older adult. It is rare in today's world to find an entire family living in the same town. More often, adult children are spread across the country. Most are willing to make arrangements for time off work, child care, and travel to participate in a well-planned family intervention. If someone important to your team can't travel, they can participate long distance by letter or telephone.

The number of people on your team should be determined by evaluating the needs of the older adult. The following suggestions are based upon the assumption that you'll use a loving approach to intervention as described in the next chapter. If the older adult has problems with dementia, use a smaller team. Too many people may confuse the older adult with cognitive problems. Late onset alcoholics (who develop the disease after the age of fifty) respond more favorably to a smaller team—of three to five people—due to shame issues. Early onset alcoholics (who have been alcoholic since young or middle adulthood) are more resistant to accepting help, so larger teams help break through denial. These are guidelines, not steadfast rules. Determine the size of your team based on your older adult's situation and your family relationships. We've done interventions with large sibling groups who had strong, loving relationships with their older parent. Rather than eliciting shame, having all the adult children present was a necessary show of support and love.

It is important that all team members keep the intervention planning confidential. Some people think that forewarning the alcoholic is a way of helping him. Instead, they unknowingly collaborate with the addiction. Advance information about a family intervention raises the alcoholic's defense mechanisms, creates an impenetrable fortress to protect the disease, and keeps relatives and friends away. Someone who will notify the alcoholic beforehand should not be on the team.

Some people thwart the family's attempt to get the older adult sober because they like drinking with the alcoholic. These people are almost always alcoholic themselves. After Gary's wife died, his alcoholism escalated. Alice, an alcoholic friend, became his regular drinking buddy. They drank together every night, and they eventually married. As the alcoholism progressed, Gary began drinking in the mornings. His children decided to intervene. They didn't include Alice on the team, because she'd warn Gary. Alice's life with Gary revolved around alcohol, and she didn't want to lose her drinking partner. Instead, the adult children consulted with a professional interventionist to learn how to successfully help their dad without enlisting Alice.

Some family members are skeptical. They don't believe anything can help the alcoholic. They believe you can't help alcoholics until they want help. The rationale is that family and friends must step back and allow alcoholics to experience years of trouble until they reach out for help on their own. But, while waiting for the alcoholic to hit bottom, the family hits bottom, too. Older adults left to hit bottom usually die before they ask for help. The humane thing to do is to *raise the bottom* by using the power of the group in a loving family intervention.

If someone says it's impossible to help the older adult until he wants help, challenge the myth. Ask this question: "If the alcoholic won't accept help until he wants help, what will make him want help?" When you add this simple question—*what makes him want help?*—you force people to think differently about the problem. When people begin asking what it takes to get an alcoholic to want help, they open the door to possibilities and opportunity.

Oftentimes, the nonalcoholic spouse avoids discussing how to help the alcoholic spouse. The older spouse comes from a generation that believes you keep marital problems private, don't burden your children with your troubles, and learn to cope on your own. The nonalcoholic spouse often "manages" the problem by rationing the alcoholic's daily intake of alcohol and tracking down and emptying bottles hidden around the house. The spouses of alcoholics also resign themselves to living with the drinking problem and resist "rocking the boat" at this late stage of life. As a rule, a spouse changes his or her mind once a serious crisis occurs in the alcoholic's life. Crisis, in essence, is first intervening upon the nonalcoholic spouse. Adult children can use a crisis to convince their reluctant parent it is time to get help for the alcoholic parent.

A family member may become openly hostile to the idea of helping the older adult. In most families, there is at least one person who, after being hurt repeatedly by the alcoholic, is angry and fed up. For example, Tony took the brunt of his father's drinking problem as he was growing up. His father, now seventy years old, was alcoholic when Tony was still in grade school. Tony was the target of his dad's drunken wrath. His dad sometimes whipped Tony with a belt and often humiliated him with verbal assaults. Tony never forgave him. When Tony's sisters asked him to help intervene on their dad, now suffering from cirrhosis, Tony became indignant. He rattled off all the reasons their dad didn't deserve his help. Tony's sisters let him vent his feelings without interrupting or disagreeing. They took time to listen and empathize with Tony, and they acknowledged his anger. They then said: "I know you're frustrated and angry with Dad. You have every right to feel the way you do. But maybe we can heal our family if we work together to get Dad into treatment. We can't change the past, but maybe by taking positive action, we can change our future. We can't lose by investigating the possibilities."

Remember that alcoholism inflicts deep wounds. Don't add to someone's hurt by minimizing his or her pain. Let people tell you why they don't want to help the older adult or the reasons they think it's a hopeless cause. It is okay for them to be reluctant. This is their starting point. They're telling you they need more time to think about what you are asking them to do. So, don't force anyone to make fast commitments. Instead, ask if they're willing to learn what the family can do. Once everyone has more information, the family can begin discussing the next best step. As writer Eugene F. Ware wisely said, "All glory comes from daring to begin."

⚓

Forget What You Think You Know

Ninety-five percent of the assumptions about intervention are wrong. Intervention isn't confrontation, ambush, or trickery. It isn't deception or chicanery. It isn't a free-for-all or a brawl. Family intervention is a finely choreographed combination of love and honesty that cracks through an older adult's denial while preserving his dignity. After an intervention, we've heard many relatives and friends say, "That was so beautiful, I wish my family would do an intervention on me even though I'm not alcoholic!"

A loving approach to intervention is important when intervening on older adults. Filled with intense feelings of shame, they drop their defenses more easily when the team uses love as its collective power, not toughness. An African proverb calls on us to "hold a true friend with both hands." In a loving intervention, we hold the older adult with both hands while we initiate a turning point in his life.

In the 1960s, Dr. Vernon E. Johnson, an Episcopal priest, developed the techniques for family intervention. He held the belief that all people suffering from progressive and fatal diseases needed treatment at the earliest possible moment, and alcoholics were no exception. A recovering alcoholic himself, Dr. Johnson would ask, "Why are alcoholics left to suffer so long?" In his book *I'll Quit Tomorrow*, he explains how the alcoholic's cry for help is unheard or misunderstood, but there nonetheless. He writes: "Whether or not you are able to hear a cry for help, it's there, and intervention is absolutely necessary. The real reason we intervene is that spontaneous insight is impossible. . . . We believe in intervention because a person's life is in danger. It is as necessary as surgery when peritonitis is inevitable. The chief misconception is that spontaneous insight may occur."

Dr. Johnson's intervention method asks each team member to compile a list of incidents and problems directly related to the alcoholic's drinking or drug use. During the intervention, each person begins with a few words of love and concern, and then reads his or her list to the alcoholic. After all letters are read, the team asks the alcoholic to accept help and presents the alcoholic with treatment options. This method focuses almost entirely on presenting one example after another of the difficulties the drinking has caused the alcoholic and his family.

This "laundry list" approach can be too harsh for older adults, and a preferable, gentler version of Dr. Johnson's intervention techniques has been developed.

The "love first" approach is described in the book *Love First: A New Approach to Intervention for Alcoholism and Drug Addiction*: "Through our work in intervention, we have found that love is a powerful force when confronting addiction. In the past, expressions of love were delegated to a few brief sentences during an intervention. We've learned that when we expand the role of love, it is love, rather than toughness, that first breaks through denial. . . . Many people have heard of *tough love* where tough comes first; this [method] puts *love first*."

This more loving approach asks each person on the team to write a letter to the older adult. Each letter has three parts. The first and longest part is a message of love. Without mentioning the alcoholism, this section of the letter is devoted to telling the alcoholic how much she is loved and respected. Just as the alcoholic is bracing herself for the worst, she hears testimonials about what a wonderful wife, mother, sister, aunt, grandmother, and friend she's been to the people in the room. Relatives and friends recall cherished memories from days gone by, recount times when the older adult helped them when they were down, and describe the older adult's best qualities. The love message is detailed and sincere. Few people can read their word of tribute without crying, and the older adult cries along with them.

The second part of the letter addresses the addiction to alcohol or mood-altering medicines. This part of the letter is specific, but short. Each family member writes about two or three incidents they've witnessed firsthand. Words such as *alcoholic* and *addict* are avoided. Statements about the chemical dependency include the words *disease* and *medical problem*. No one resorts to anger, judgment, or resentment, and facts are expressed in a loving tone. Keep this section brief to avoid creating unnecessary feelings of shame. But brevity is not a reason to gloss over details.

The "addiction" part of the letter illustrates to older adults what they cannot see for themselves—how alcohol is changing them. Sometimes team members are afraid to be honest about the addiction, but the older adult needs honesty. As Roman orator and poet Marcus Tullius Cicero asks: "Where is there dignity unless there is honesty?"

The third part of the letter is the conclusion. This section tells the older adult what you are asking him to do. A typical conclusion is: "Mom, I could never live with myself if I stood by and did nothing to help you. You are my best friend, and I can't bear losing you to this disease. Before Dad died, he asked me to promise that I'd watch over you. Today I promise *you* I will stand by you and do my part to help. I'm asking you to take my hand and accept help. Will you accept the help we are all offering you today?"

Put aside everything you think you know about intervention and begin anew. With an updated education, you can make a well-informed decision. In the next chapter, you'll read letters written to older alcoholics for actual family interventions. They illustrate better than any narrative how loving an intervention can be while still being honest.

⚓

Actual Intervention Letters

The following letters were written for an older parent or grandparent and used in real interventions. They are examples of a *love first* approach and an excellent guide for anyone writing a letter for an intervention. The names and some details have been changed in each letter to protect the anonymity of the older adult and the writer.

A forty-year-old daughter wrote the following letter to her sixty-eight-year-old mother. It is a perfect example of writing with sensitivity to the values of the older adult:

Dear Mom,

From an early age, you taught me values and virtues. I remember when I was five years old, and I stole gum from Kaner's Corner Store. You took me to confess my misdeed and pay the storekeeper. It was a hard lesson at the time, but you taught me about honesty. I never stole again. Another time when I was in trouble, you took me to apologize to Mr. Bennett after he kept the ball that went into his yard, and I called him a name. You had him over to dinner after that, and we became very good friends.

You taught me to be kind and compassionate to others, to put myself in other people's shoes, and to treat them as I would like to be treated. You patterned for me a gregarious, friendly, loving person to all people. You never met a stranger.

You always thought of others before yourself. You taught me to respect all people regardless of their race, color, or position in life. You taught me to respect my elders, the people in authority, and our government. You taught me to be thankful for whatever I received, and to take care of my possessions.

Dad always complimented you on your beauty. But your beauty was not only outward. You used to say, "Clean up in the morning, put on your best face, and then don't think about it again."

You were always helping other people—neighbors, Granny and Granddaddy, Mitch, and Snookey. After Aunt Cecilia died and Uncle Randy couldn't care for Cousin Al, you took him in and raised him like one of your own. You took Meals on Wheels to people who were in need. You selflessly took care of our dad when he was dying of cancer and, most recently, Uncle Phil. You saw to his every need up to the very end.

You are so much fun. You always played games with us kids. You made every holiday special and memorable. You made gourmet meals and taught us good table manners. You taught us to always address our elders by saying, "Yes sir" and "no sir" and "yes ma'am" and "no ma'am." You taught us work ethics. You always said, "A job worth doing is worth doing well." Cleaning my room was an all-day event!

When you saw I had a need, you immediately came to my aid. Many times when I was ill, you stayed up all night to care for me. When I had a fever, nothing felt as comforting as your cool hand. When I had a problem in school, you were on top of it. You helped my reading tremendously with your many lessons. I went from an F to a B in chemistry and loved my teacher after you went with me to talk to him.

You are such a dear mother. I love you, I respect you, and I am so thankful for you. You deserve the best in life.

When Dad had his biopsy, you alerted us kids, and we all came to be with you and Dad. When Dad was told it was cancer, you took him right away to the best hospital for cancer treatment. You stood by him untiringly. That's what loved ones do, and you patterned this for me.

Mom, now you have a disease. It's robbing you of life, dignity, and relationships. Alcohol has taken over your life. You stay at home by yourself more and more these days. You tell me you like being alone, but I know your companion is alcohol. Your disease has reached a point where you sit at home and drink alone. You've told me you're depressed. Alcohol is a depressant, and most people suffering from alcohol dependence become depressed. You and I have talked about these things.

You seem happiest when you visit one of us kids, but when you return home, you're alone again, and the alcohol takes over. It breaks my heart to see bruises, burns, and the marks of falls and injuries on you. It also hurts me to see how swollen your legs are from edema caused by alcohol. They look so uncomfortable, painful, and discolored. You told me of falling and bruising your face recently—that pretty face.

You are such a vital person in our lives and the lives of your grandchildren. I love you so much and want to encourage you to get help for this disease that is so destructive in your life. I was with you when we sought help for the disease of cancer that attacked Dad's body. I want to help you by taking you right now to the best treatment center available for treating this disease in older adults. You'll be with people your own age.

Betty Ford received help for her affliction with alcohol after President Ford and their children met with her, just like we're doing here today. Many wonderful people like you have sought help and have overcome this disease.

I can no longer stand by and watch this disease take over my mom. I am here to help you just as I was moved to help Dad when he got cancer. That's what loved ones do; you patterned this for me. Mom, will you go with us now?

> Love,
> Your daughter,
> Jackie

The next letter was written by a college-aged granddaughter to her grandmother:

Dear Granny,

You and I have always had a special bond. We like to sit and talk about life and philosophy, and it always seems we end up solving the problems of the world. I can always count on you for anything and everything. I think you know you are like a second mother to me. I told you just the other day how much Christmastime means to me, and I thanked you for providing me with so many warm memories. As far back as I can remember, every stay at your house was a joy for me. I know you always go out of your way to make things special for me.

I love you so much—it's more than love, even—you're just more important to me than you could possibly imagine. You and

Granddad keep this family together; you make us whole. I am here for you today because I want you to be healthy. While I may speak of the past, this is about the here and now—today, and our future together as a family. So, please know this is not meant to hurt you, but to bring our family together with love.

Granny, when you are sober, you are as reliable as a clock. Since you have long periods when you do not drink, I can let myself ignore the fact that you suffer from this disease and just concentrate on the good times. I always think, "Maybe she won't drink again. Maybe that last time was her last."

Last spring, when a binge landed you in the hospital, Mom, Dad, Janie, and I decided for about the third time that we were going to do *something* to get you help. But then you got pneumonia, and that allowed me to forget about the drinking and concentrate on other things. It is easy for me to pretend nothing is wrong—especially a week or so after a drinking binge. It is more comfortable for me to concentrate on the good stuff.

Last April, after I got back from visiting you and Granddad, my mom told me you drank again. I was so surprised and all those old feelings I push out of my mind came rushing back. They always come back when I hear about a binge. Questions run through my mind: "What made her do it this time?" "How bad was it?" "How long did it last?" "How far and where did she drive?" "Did she hurt herself?" "Is she at home or in the hospital?" "Is Granddad okay?"

You may not know this, but I usually find out when you've gone on a binge, even a small one. Mom might say, "We think Granny's drinking." It isn't a secret. Everyone knows, everyone hurts, it's on everyone's mind.

The Thursday you started drinking this last time, I remember coming home and finding you sitting in the kitchen. Granddad was doing the dishes, and you and I had a great conversation for about five minutes before I realized your laugh was a little too hearty, you were talking a little too much. The realization came upon me like a slap in the face. I actually backed away from you physically and could only respond in one-word sentences. I just wanted to get out of there and forget what I was seeing. When Mom told me you had gotten drunk, it felt like a punch in the stomach.

I don't have many memories of witnessing your binges. Instead, what I have is a feeling that is always with me. It is a fear that nags at me: "Someday, Granny is going to die from alcohol." A lot of the time, I rely on my denial so I can go on without going crazy from that thought. A picture that stays in my head is you lying dead in a snowdrift, having passed out after a binge. I read about a woman in her forties dying that way a few years ago. The image stays with me. Granny, I don't want to have those kinds of thoughts about you.

A few days ago, I started thinking about the fact that despite this devastating, debilitating disease you've been suffering with for nearly half a century, you've accomplished so much and deserve the love and respect of so many. You're really quite amazing. It takes a strong woman to do what you have done for so long in the face of a disease that kills so many. I know you can beat this disease, but that is not accomplished alone. If it could be done alone, you would have done it by now. But no one recovers alone. It requires reaching out to others.

So will you please accept the help we are offering? The help I am asking you to take? We are together as a family, and I promise I will do my part. Please take the first step toward recovery with us today.

Love,
Miranda

Learn about Family Intervention

A good intervention starts with good information. Your team can choose from several educational resources. Team members should use the same resource, so everyone works together and can easily discuss what they've learned.

Families usually start in one of two ways: They hire a professional interventionist or read a book on intervention. If your older adult is in crisis, and you want to intervene immediately, working with a professional from the start is advisable. An interventionist can train a family quickly. Emergency interventions can take place in less than two days after first contacting the interventionist. Most families need two weeks or more to plan an intervention without professional help.

Family intervention techniques were originally designed for families to use on their own, but intervention has evolved into a profession. This has led to an ongoing debate about whether families can intervene on alcoholics without professional help. We believe some families can proceed without an interventionist. We've talked with many people who have successfully done this. Dr. Johnson, in his book *Intervention,* writes: "You may believe that only the experts—physicians, psychiatrists, chemical dependency counselors—are equipped and able to help the chemically dependent person. That is not necessarily the case . . . *anyone who sincerely wants to help, can help.* You do not need a clinical background or special expertise." However, before families embark on this endeavor, they must educate themselves, follow the directions closely, and pay close attention to the details.

Intervention is an emotionally charged time for families, and your team may feel more comfortable working with a professional. To locate an interventionist in your hometown, ask a local alcohol and drug treatment center for a referral. If there are no interventionists in your area, nationally known treatment centers maintain lists of interventionists who work throughout the United States and Canada. The Hanley-Hazelden Center, known for its older adult treatment program, provides names of interventionists who travel nationwide and specialize in older adults. For a referral, call 800-444-7008.

There are circumstances when an intervention should not be undertaken without an attending professional. Dr. Johnson recommends using a professional when the alcoholic has a history of mental illness, violent behavior, deep depression, or use of several different types of mood-altering drugs unidentifiable by the family.

Additionally, involve a professional if the alcoholic has had several previous treatments followed by relapse, has had a history of suicide attempts, or has recently threatened suicide. If family relationships have greatly deteriorated with the alcoholic, a professional may be necessary. We also suggest hiring a professional if the older adult is showing signs of dementia.

Books are excellent education tools and an inexpensive way to get started. After reading a book, the team can decide if intervention is the next best step for the family and if hiring an interventionist is necessary. Intervention books are available online at the Hazelden Bookplace by logging on to www.hazeldenbookplace.org. Click onto "Helpful Books," then select "Intervention." You'll find books on family intervention for less than $15.00. You can also search recovery sections of bookstores and public libraries.

Books are a good first step for reluctant family members who aren't ready to commit to the intervention process. Books give them more information. Adult children can use books as a first step with parents who are hesitant about doing an intervention. You can also ask family members to review information on the Internet.

Intervention fees are not covered by health insurance policies. If the cost of hiring an interventionist is a financial hardship for your family and you believe you need professional guidance, there are affordable options. Instead of using an interventionist to facilitate the entire intervention process, schedule a brief consultation session once everyone has finished reading about intervention. If the interventionist is located out of town, arrange a conference call or use a speaker phone so all team members can participate. Asking questions specific to your situation may give you the additional information you need to proceed on your own. To get questions answered at no cost, Hazelden provides a live Internet chat on intervention every Tuesday night at nine o'clock eastern time. The chat is hosted by a professional interventionist. Log on to http://sites.chatspace.com:8189/.

If circumstances dictate that you use a professional interventionist, but your family can't afford the expenditure, ask a clergyperson or a lay minister to chair the intervention. Provide a copy of the intervention book your team is using and include him or her in your planning meetings.

⚏

Plan, Plan, Plan

Eleanor Roosevelt once said, "It takes as much energy to wish as it does to plan." People who spend years wishing the alcoholic would get sober are surprised to see what some careful planning can accomplish. The success of an intervention is intricately tied to how it is implemented.

Once you and your team are educated, either by working with a professional or reading a book, methodically follow the directions. This is not a time for shortcuts. Following are the most important initial steps in planning your intervention:

- *Gather and record information about the older adult.* Different people have different information, so ask everyone on the team to participate. This information will help you decide the treatment needs of the older adult. When you contact a treatment center, the admissions staff will ask you for much of this information as part of a preintake assessment.

- *Set a date and time for the intervention.* Once you have a date set, work backward as you plan the intervention. If you decide to do the intervention Saturday morning at nine o'clock, then plan your rehearsal session for Friday, and so forth. Remember to choose a time when the alcoholic is most likely to be sober and available.

- *Determine financial resources for treatment.* Gather information about insurance policies, Medicare, and personal resources to pay for treatment. Your resources determine what treatment programs you can access for the older adult.

- *Evaluate treatment centers.* Using the treatment center evaluation questions in this book, determine the best treatment options for the older adult. Ask about admissions requirements and costs.

- *Choose a treatment program.* Once you've selected a treatment facility, complete the preintake assessment and make financial arrangements. Set up an admissions appointment for the day of the intervention. If the facility is in another city or state, make travel reservations. Keep the length of time between the intervention and admission into treatment (or departure of the airplane) to a minimum. For example, if the intervention is scheduled for nine in the morning, combine the length of time for the intervention with the travel time to determine the best time for the appointment. If you estimate your intervention will take thirty minutes, build in another thirty minutes for the older adult's questions or objections. Then add driving time. If the drive is one hour, you'll schedule the admission for eleven o'clock. The more time the older adult has between the intervention and the admission, the more time he has to change his mind.

- *Prepare for the possibility that the older adult will refuse treatment.* When younger people refuse help during an intervention, the team presents *bottom lines*—ways they will no longer enable the disease. A boss may say: "If you choose not to go to treatment, I can no longer ignore your poor job performance. I'll have to take you off the payroll." A wife may say: "I can no longer subject the children to your alcoholic behaviors. If you choose to stay sick, you cannot live in the house." Families intervening on older adults usually don't have the same kinds of bottom lines. Because older adults are often retired and financially secure, there is little or no leverage for the family to use on them. But family relationships carry a great deal of influence with older adults. A bottom line for an older adult might be: "Mom, your grandkids love you, but your drinking scares them and puts them in an unsafe situation. If you decide not to get help, the kids won't be able to visit. I don't want that to happen. Won't you please get help instead?" Never choose a bottom line that will endanger the older adult, such as eliminating legitimate caregiving— "I refuse to drive you to your doctor appointments," for example.

As you plan your intervention, use a checklist to monitor your progress. One member of the team, designated as the detail person, checks off each task as it is completed. Review the checklist the day before the intervention so you're certain nothing is left undone. You want the intervention to move forward as smoothly as possible. Below is a sample checklist. Don't plan an intervention using the checklist alone.

The Checklist

☐ Bring together three to eight people who are important to the older adult and are willing to learn how to help.

☐ If using a book as an intervention resource, read the book in its entirety for a precise education on how to motivate an addicted loved one to accept help.

- ☐ If using an interventionist, call a treatment center for a referral.
- ☐ Set up a planning meeting to discuss moving forward with the intervention.
- ☐ Use "Collecting Helpful Information," provided in this book, to record and organize information.
- ☐ Choose a detail person to record information and monitor preparations.
- ☐ Choose a team chairperson to preside at the intervention. If you are working with an interventionist, he or she can serve as chairperson.
- ☐ Discuss the importance of not alerting the alcoholic to the intervention plans.
- ☐ List ways you've tried to help the alcoholic that may have actually enabled the addiction.
- ☐ Put in writing all the negative consequences caused by the addiction. Refer to "Signs of Alcoholism and Drug Abuse in Older People" at the back of this book.
- ☐ Write a one- to two-page letter to the alcoholic, using a loving approach for older adults. Shorten the length of your letters if the older adult is suffering from dementia or a short attention span.
- ☐ Read your letters to each other, editing out anger, blame, and judgment.
- ☐ Determine bottom lines, and write them down on a separate page. Bottom lines for older adults are different than for younger adults.
  - ☐ Test each other's willingness to follow through with the bottom lines.
  - ☐ Differentiate between bottom lines and legitimate caregiving.
- ☐ Identify financial resources for covering treatment costs.

- [ ] Evaluate treatment centers.
    - [ ] Do they offer older adult services?
    - [ ] If not, can they tailor their existing program to the special needs of the older adult?
- [ ] Set a date, time, and place for the rehearsal and the intervention.
- [ ] Choose a treatment center, answer its preintake questions, make an appointment for admission, and finalize financial arrangements.
- [ ] Make airline reservations if the treatment center is out of state.
- [ ] Create a plan likely to guarantee the alcoholic's presence at the intervention.
- [ ] Identify objections the alcoholic may use to avoid or postpone treatment, then formulate your answers.
- [ ] Pack a suitcase using the guidelines provided by the treatment staff.
- [ ] Determine who should drive the alcoholic from the intervention to the treatment center or airport. Who will fly with the older adult to the treatment center?
- [ ] Compile a list of all prescribed medications the alcoholic is presently using.
    - [ ] Make a copy for the doctor at the treatment center.
    - [ ] Pack all medications and give them to the nursing staff.
- [ ] Rehearse the intervention.
    - [ ] Decide where each person will sit, including the alcoholic.
    - [ ] Discuss the order in which you'll read your letters.
    - [ ] Find a discreet place to park your cars.
    - [ ] Script the chairperson's introduction and closing.
    - [ ] Review objections and answers.
    - [ ] Call and confirm the appointment at the treatment center.
    - [ ] Rehearse the intervention exactly as you'll do the real thing.
- [ ] Plan to be at the intervention location thirty minutes before the alcoholic is expected to arrive.

☐ If the intervention is taking place at the alcoholic's home, arrive as a complete group.

☐ After the intervention, call the admissions staff and let them know whether or not the alcoholic has agreed to treatment.

☐ Collect all intervention letters and send them to the alcoholic's treatment counselor.

☐ Sign up for the treatment center's family program, if it provides one.

☐ Locate an Al-Anon or Families Anonymous meeting near your home or office.

Adapted with permission from Love First: A New Approach to Intervention from Alcoholism and Drug Addiction *by Jeff Jay and Debra Jay (Center City, Minn.: Hazelden, 2000).*

⚓

A Dramatization of an Intervention

Eighty-five percent of properly implemented interventions are successful at motivating the older alcoholic to accept help. Most family interventions unfold almost exactly as this one does.

Characters

BETTY, a sixty-nine-year-old with an alcohol and tranquilizer addiction

CAROL, her forty-eight-year-old daughter

PETER, her forty-six-year-old son

TIFFANY, her twenty-one-year-old granddaughter

CAROLINE, her seventy-four-year-old sister

DR. BELL, her physician, unable to attend

The intervention is taking place in the living room of Peter's house. Since Betty's husband passed away, she and Peter have

been very close. Peter takes care of all the maintenance and re-
pairs on her house and checks on Betty several times a week.
Peter has the most leverage with Betty because she depends upon
his help. Selecting Peter's house for the intervention is an unspo-
ken reminder of this, and it can influence Betty's decision.

Betty's granddaughter Tiffany is home from college, so Peter
invited Betty over for a get-together after church. Betty's daughter,
Carol, offered to drive her over to Peter's house. Everyone else ar-
rived thirty minutes before Betty and Carol were expected.

Betty's sister, Caroline, flew in from out of state to participate in
the intervention. Betty isn't expecting her sister to be at the get-
together. This will be the first time Betty and Caroline have seen
each other in almost two years, but they stay in close contact by
phone.

The day before, the family rehearsed the intervention. They de-
termined where each person, including Betty, would sit. They
decided the best order for reading the letters. They practiced read-
ing all letters out loud just as they would in the actual interven-
tion. They prepared for possible objections. Peter was selected as
chairman and will preside over the intervention and answer any
objections.

Betty and Carol are expected in fifteen minutes. Everybody
takes his or her seat. All beverages, food, and cigarettes are re-
moved from the room. Pets are put outside. Telephones, cell
phones, and beepers are turned off. The team waits for the sound
of Carol's car. They hear a car pull up in the driveway. The door-
bell rings. Peter opens the door.

BETTY: [handing Peter a plate of cookies] How are you, Dear? I
made Tiffany's favorite.
PETER: [bending over to kiss Betty on the cheek] Thanks, Mom.
She'll love these. Come on in. Everyone's in the living room.

Carol walks past Betty and Peter, and heads for her seat in the liv-
ing room with the rest of the team.

BETTY: [arriving in the living room; shocked] Caroline, what in heaven's sake are you doing here? No one told me!

PETER: [lovingly puts his hand on Betty's shoulder and looks her straight in the eye] Mom, we all love you so much. We have something important we want to share with you, and Aunt Caroline wanted to be here, too. Come sit down between Tiffany and me.

Peter gently guides Betty toward the couch where Tiffany is seated.

BETTY: [with concern] Is everyone all right? Is something wrong?

Betty sits down and takes Tiffany's hand. Tiffany gives her grandmother's hand a little squeeze and then lets go.

PETER: [seated and turning toward Betty] Mom, we're all fine. We've all taken the time to write you a letter, and we'd like you to listen as we read each one.

BETTY: [hesitant] Okay. But what is this about?

PETER: [staying on message rather than getting sidetracked by Betty's question] Well, why don't we listen to Caroline's letter?

Betty turns toward her sister and smiles. Caroline looks at Betty and smiles back. She begins to read her letter.

CAROLINE: Dear Bet, you are my darling little sister. I remember when Mother and Dad brought you home from the hospital. You were swaddled in a pink blanket and looked like a little doll. I had asked our parents for a sister for so long, I couldn't believe they finally got one for me. That's what I thought. I truly believed they went out and got you just for me. I was overjoyed.

There was never any sibling rivalry between the two of us. Maybe that's because there were enough years between us; we didn't need to compete. Of course, in my teenage years, I couldn't keep you out of my stuff. Remember when you got ahold of my lipstick and smeared it all over your face? Mother gave you a good scolding, but

I heard her and Daddy laugh about it later. Then there was the time I was on the front porch smooching with my high school sweetheart, Tommy O'Brady. I thought he was the cat's pajamas, remember? Well, you were spying on us and thought it would be funny to tell Dad I needed him out on the front porch. When Dad showed up, Tommy jumped up and took off so fast he almost fell down the steps. He could never look Dad in the eye again. Mother and Dad didn't know whether to yell at you or yell at me. Looking back, it was darn funny, but at the time I could've brained you.

Bet, you've been the greatest blessing in my life. You have a fabulous sense of humor. You can make me laugh more than anybody else. We always have such fun when we're together. And you also have a generous, compassionate heart. I can always depend on you to be there for me, and that's why I'm here today. I'm here for you.

I've been aware for some time that you have a disease. It's the disease of alcohol dependence, and it runs in our family. Grandma Patterson had it and died a terrible death by cirrhosis. Cousin Jane had a problem, too, as you know. But ever since she went in for treatment, she's done well. This is a disease, Bet, and it requires medical attention just like any other disease.

When I call you on the phone these days, I call early in the day. I know if I call after four or five in the afternoon, you'll be slurring your words. Last month I called you at seven-thirty in the evening to tell you Olivia had a stroke. When I called three days later to tell you she died, you said, "Why didn't anyone tell me Olivia had a stroke? The family must think I'm terrible for not calling to find out how she was doing." When I said I had talked to you the night it happened, stunned silence came from your end of the line. You then said, "That's impossible," and rushed to get off the phone. I knew you were embarrassed and trying to cover for yourself.

Bet, I am here to ask you to get the help that is available for this disease of alcohol dependence. I'm here to stand by you all the way. I can't lose my sister and best friend. Not when you are suffering from a very treatable disease. Please accept the help we are offering you today. Love, your sister, Caroline.

BETTY: [sniffling] Thank you, Caroline.

Peter glances at Carol to cue her that it's her turn to read her letter. She turns to her mother and begins crying. After a few moments, she regains her composure and begins reading.

CAROL: Dear Mom, as a kid, I was always so proud you were my mother. Other girls used to talk about how embarrassed they were by their mothers, but I never felt that way about you. In fact, all the kids liked to hang out at our house because you made everyone feel welcome.

Once I became a mother, I realized how much I learned from you. Being mothered by you taught me how to be a good mother to my children. My kids turned out so great, in no small way, due to you. And the kids love you so much. But, like myself, they are worried about your health. The twins asked me the other day, "Mom, why isn't anyone helping Grandma? Everyone knows she needs help, but no one is doing anything." I promised the girls we would help you. They wanted me to tell you they love you. I love you, too.

Carol continues her letter, giving three examples of how Betty's alcohol and tranquilizer dependence has caused problems in her life. She concludes the letter by asking her to accept help. Betty, crying, searches for a tissue in her pocketbook. Peter nods at Tiffany, Betty's granddaughter, to cue her that it's her turn.

TIFFANY: [crying] Grams, I love you so much. You always bring me love and goodies. When I was little, you'd always bring me Cracker Jacks and Circus Peanuts. You'd take me to Sunrise Bakery to buy me glazed donuts and elephant ears. Or we'd go to Steven's Coffee Shop for a piece of pie, and you'd tell me all the latest news about everyone. You never talked to me like a kid, but like a friend. Every

minute I spent with you was special. You have the greatest personality in the world.

When my parents got divorced, you were the one who kept my
world steady. You were always there to listen. You said to me: "Don't
take on your parent's problems. They belong to them, not you. Your
only job is to be a kid." I never told you, but that helped me so
much. Now I want to help you, because I can see that you are suffering from a disease.

*Tiffany finishes her letter by sharing times she has seen alcohol
and tranquilizers affect her grandmother, and she asks Betty to
accept help today. Betty is crying and reaches over to hug Tiffany.
Peter turns to his mother, gives her a reassuring smile, and begins
to read his letter.*

PETER: [takes a deep breath] Dear Mom, have I told you lately just
how much I love you? I guess I always assume you know, but I don't
tell you nearly enough. Mom, I love you. [Peter breaks down crying]
You've always been my biggest cheerleader. When I had trouble
reading, and the teachers labeled me a slow learner, you said, "I
know my son. He may not be able to read, but he's not slow." You
took me to specialist after specialist until finally I was diagnosed
with dyslexia. You said, "Now that we can name it, we can overcome it." And—with your strength and determination behind me—
overcome it, I did. When I graduated from dental school, it was a
tribute to the mother who never stopped believing in her son. My
life would not be what it is today if it weren't for you.

When Carrie filed for divorce, I was devastated. Again, you were
by my side. Always fair, you told me I needed to accept my respon-
sibility for my part in our problems and not allow myself to become
bitter toward Carrie's part. You said, "Sad, brokenhearted, even
mad is okay. But you have a daughter, and you can't afford bitter."
And, of course, you were right.

Mom, when Dad was dying, the hardest thing for him was leaving you alone in this world. He worried about how you'd make out without him. I promised him I would watch over you. I know he's looking down on us right now. As hard as this is for me, I know he'd want me to be honest with you about how alcohol and prescription drugs are hurting you. Dr. Bell is concerned, too. He didn't realize you were getting tranquilizers from two doctors and mixing them with alcohol. He's written a letter recommending you get treatment to overcome this problem. It's a medical issue, and it's dangerous to stop without proper detoxification. This is what he has written.

Peter reads the letter from Dr. Bell to his mother, and then resumes reading his own letter.

Mom, I've come by on Saturdays and found you intoxicated at two o'clock in the afternoon. You would never choose this for yourself. The alcohol is running the show and robbing you of your dignity. You've been meticulous your whole life, but lately your appearance is suffering. I've seen bruises and burns on you so many times, it's becoming normal. You always come up with some excuse, but I know the truth. It isn't uncommon for older people to become chemically dependent due to changes in the aging body. Mom, it is not your fault you have this disease, but you must get help. You are losing your memory, and I question if you can continue living alone if you let this go on. We've found an excellent treatment facility for people in your age group. The facility is beautiful. They have gardens, a swimming pool, and a small chapel. We've made all the arrangements. I have the plane tickets. You, Aunt Caroline, and I will fly there today. Aunt Caroline and I are staying through the weekend to attend the family education program they offer. Mom, come with us today to get the help you need. Love, your son, Peter.

Betty looks down at her hands for a minute and says nothing. The team remains silent. Then Peter turns to his mother, takes her hand, and looks her in the eye.

PETER: Mother, will you accept the help we are offering you today?

BETTY: Where is it you want me to go?

PETER: Here's a brochure. We did extensive research to find the best program for you. It's designed for people in their sixties and seventies who suffer from this same disease.

BETTY: [looking at the brochure] How long do I have to stay?

PETER: We want you to follow their recommendations. Most people stay four weeks.

BETTY: I suppose you're right. I have been experiencing some problems. It's been hard since your father passed. But I think I could handle this on my own.

PETER: [calmly, but firmly] Mother, as Dr. Bell wrote in his letter, this requires professional attention. You can endanger your life by going off alcohol and pills without medical help. And to stay off, you need treatment. Doing it on your own is not an option. It isn't safe. It is a recipe for disaster. Come with us today, and take care of this in the right way.

BETTY: [long pause] Okay, I'll go.

Peter reaches over, crying, and gives his mother a big hug. Everyone begins to cry and gets up to give Betty a hug.

⚜

Another Ending

About 15 percent of family interventions end with a refusal to accept treatment. However, many older adults who refuse treatment at the time of the intervention accept help at a later date.

BETTY: [caustically] I am not going to go into a treatment center. I'll agree that alcohol may be giving me a little trouble, but it's nothing I can't correct on my own. As far as the tranquilizers go, I don't care what Dr. Bell says. They come from doctors. They are medicine for my anxiety. You know I can't sleep since your dad died. How do any of you know what I go through? How can you possibly know?

PETER: [calmly] Today, we are talking about what we are all witnessing—your chemical dependency. Your doctor recognizes it, and each of us in this room recognizes it. But the person suffering from the problem is the last to see it, so we understand why this is difficult for you. That's why we've come together as a family to talk honestly and directly with you about getting help.

BETTY: [sarcastically] I don't need help from anybody.

PETER: [remaining calm] Mother, we've taken care of everything. You don't need to worry about anything. It's all taken care of. Aunt Caroline and I are ready to go with you today. It is the right thing to do. Please accept our help.

BETTY: [stubbornly] I don't care if it's the right thing, I'm not going. That's final.

PETER: [maintaining a loving, even tone] Mother, if you choose not to get help for this disease of chemical dependency, we have made decisions not to do things that will help you stay sick. We also will take care of ourselves, because this is emotionally very hard on each of us. We'd like to share our decisions with you. Caroline?

CAROLINE: Betty, you and I live a long distance from one another, but we talk on the phone often. You call me at night after you've been drinking at least once a week. I am no longer going to talk if you sound intoxicated, and I'll be honest with you the next day about how it makes me feel when you call me in that condition. I've pretended not to notice in the past so as not to embarrass you. Also, I've avoided making a trip to see you in the last two years because of the alcohol and pills. I've made other excuses rather than being honest with you. I promise to be honest from now on, so you know the truth. Won't you get help today, and avoid future problems?

CAROL: Mom, I know this disease affects people in a way that prevents them from seeing how serious the problem has become. I have helped you stay sick by ignoring the problem and lying for you. I've lied to the kids, saying, "We can't go to Grandma's today. She has the flu, or a headache," or I make some other excuse. I'm lying to my own children, and they know it. I lied to Mrs. Palmer last month when you were too inebriated to go to her granddaughter's baby shower. I'm not a liar, Mom. I can't do this anymore. From now on, if you are unable to see your grandchildren or meet a social obligation because you are intoxicated, I am going to be honest. I'll say to the kids, "Grandma's been drinking and taking pills, so we can't go over today." Or I'll say, "My mother regrets that she is unable to attend, but her untreated chemical dependency leads to frequent intoxication."

TIFFANY: Grandma, I love you and want you to get help. I'll support you in any way I can. I told Dad I'd fly down and go to the family program while you're there. Then we could visit. Please accept help and give me my wonderful grandma back.

PETER: Mom, I've found you passed out on several occasions and have stayed with you all night to make sure you didn't die. Each time, it was a living hell for me. Once I had to cancel my morning patients because you were so sick after a night of binge drinking. From now on, if I find you in that condition, I am calling the paramedics and having them bring you to the hospital for a drug overdose. I have already talked to all your doctors about your drug-seeking behavior. I love you too much to do anything that will make it easier for you to stay sick. But if you decide to get well, every one of us is willing to help you get better. Won't you take the step with us today and accept help?

Most people agree to treatment after hearing bottom lines. But Betty did not. She said she could handle the problem on her own. Peter asked her if she'd accept help if she tried and failed to do it on her own. She agreed to this compromise. Over the next few days, Betty tried to quit on her own, but withdrawal symptoms and cravings led her back to alcohol and pills. Three weeks later, Peter found her passed out in her living room. He called the paramedics, and they brought her to the hospital. The next day, Dr. Bell, Peter, and Carol did a short, informal intervention in the hospital. Dr. Bell told Betty she was being transferred from the hospital directly to treatment. Peter said she couldn't return home, because it was no longer safe for her to live alone. Without treatment, she would move into an assisted living facility. Betty agreed to go to treatment.

⊥⊥⊥

Understanding Treatment for Older Adults

What Exactly Is Treatment?

Treatment is a head-start program for recovery, but it isn't recovery. Recovery starts *after* people are discharged from treatment. Treatment is the beginning of the solution, not the end of the problem. People don't leave treatment "fixed." They leave knowing how to work an ongoing program of recovery.

One of the primary objectives of treatment is to break through the reoccurring denial experienced by all alcoholics. Denial doesn't end once someone is admitted into treatment—alcoholics continue to rationalize, minimize, project, and deny the seriousness of their problems. Treatment staff are trained to identify, confront, and overcome denial. Alcoholics voice their denial in the form of objections to treatment. Below are seven objections an older adult may make while in treatment:

- *I understand everything they're teaching me, so it's a waste of time to stay any longer.* The older adult is underestimating the seriousness of his addiction and the difficulty of maintaining sobriety. He believes that a short education course on addiction is sufficient.
- *I can't relate to the people here.* The older adult sets himself apart from other alcoholics. Often referred to as *terminal uniqueness* or *grandiosity*, this is a common symptom of denial.
- *I have to leave treatment because I don't like (my counselor, the food, my bed . . . and the list goes on).* Older adults who are craving alcohol or other drugs often voice discontent with aspects of the treatment facility. Those who leave treatment for these reasons usually drink shortly thereafter.
- *I'm not getting a thing out of this program.* Resistance, a form of denial, keeps older adults from participating in the program. They get nothing from the program because they refuse to put anything into it.

- *I have too many important things going on in my life to stay in treatment.* The older adult minimizes the seriousness of her addiction by focusing on other activities as more important. For instance, an alcoholic grandmother who was frequently passed out when her grandchildren visited now insists she must leave treatment to be home for her granddaughter's graduation.
- *Other people are much worse off than I am. I don't belong here.* The alcoholic is focusing on problems worse than his own as proof that he doesn't have a serious problem. This is called *comparing out*.
- *I'm not like these alcoholics; the doctor gave me those pills.* Older adults addicted to mood-altering prescription medications deny that drugs from doctors can lead to the same kind of addiction as alcohol or illicit drugs. Addiction is viewed as a moral issue or a personal weakness.

Denial is an ongoing problem in treatment. Patients, grateful for treatment one day, are determined to leave the next. Karl, a fifty-seven-year-old early onset alcoholic, came into treatment saying: "I'm so lucky to be here. This is just what I need. Alcohol has been a big problem for me." Karl's wife left him, and he wanted to save his marriage. He assured his counselor he was "ready to do whatever it takes." After a few days, Karl's emotional pain began to diminish. His wife, impressed that he was in treatment, agreed to move back home. Karl felt he'd learned a lot about alcoholism in his first few days and was convinced he'd never drink again. "I feel great," he told his counselor. "I'm ready to go home." As he felt better, Karl's denial snapped back into place. The treatment staff confronted his denial, helping him understand why he was not ready to go home. Karl stayed, but he experienced other periods of denial throughout treatment. Because of denial's persistent nature, overcoming it is an ongoing process.

Another objective of treatment is motivating patients to commit to an ongoing recovery program in Alcoholics Anonymous. Studies show that people who are sober ten years after completing treatment have one thing in common: They attend Alcoholics Anonymous. But older alcoholics in treatment routinely resist committing to Alcoholics Anonymous or other Twelve Step recovery programs. Many alcoholics believe they've learned enough in treatment to maintain sobriety. This is similar to believing a month's worth of insulin can cure diabetes for a lifetime. People who don't make a commitment to a recovery program eventually revert back to old behaviors and relapse.

Clarisa was a fifty-nine-year-old college professor addicted to alcohol and marijuana. When she entered treatment, Clarisa quickly anointed herself the "expert" and believed she knew more than her counselors did. Clarisa refused to commit to a program of recovery in Alcoholics Anonymous or to participate in an aftercare support group. Once she returned home, Clarisa abstained from alcohol, but rationalized that smoking marijuana was okay. After all, she told herself, my real problem is booze, not pot. A few months later, Clarisa decided she could have a drink or two without losing control. Six months later, Clarisa checked herself back into treatment after being suspended from her teaching position due to problems related to addiction. The clinical team worked with Clarisa to help her understand the connection between her relapse and her refusal to commit to a recovery program. She eventually admitted she needed the support of Alcoholics Anonymous to achieve long-term sobriety. When she left her second treatment, she began attending a Twelve Step program and maintained sobriety from both alcohol and marijuana.

Different types of treatment programs offer different levels of intensity and support. The most intensive level of care is residential inpatient care, where patients spend twenty-four hours a day in treatment. Inpatient programs are holistic and multidisciplinary. They treat the whole person and address all areas of the alcoholic's life—health, relationships, self-esteem, social life, spirituality, emotional wellness, grief, vocation, leisure, and mental health. The clinical team is composed of different specialists working together to determine the needs of each patient. Multidisciplinary teams include medical doctors, psychologists, nurses, chemical dependency counselors, recreation specialists, nutritionists, clergy, relaxation specialists, and family counselors.

Inpatient treatment is composed of numerous components: medical detoxification, physical examination and consultation, psychiatric evaluation, group therapy, individual counseling, educational lectures, bibliotherapy (reading assignments), specialized groups (grief, women's issues, men's issues, and so on), orientation to Alcoholics Anonymous, nutritional counseling, relaxation sessions, recreation (important for teaching alcoholics how to have fun sober), personal time, working the steps of Alcoholics Anonymous, family program, and aftercare planning.

Traditionally, inpatient programs last twenty-eight days. Studies show that most alcoholics don't have a major break in their denial system until after twenty-one days in treatment. A study by MEDSTAT, a company that specializes in health services research, found that 48 percent of people who received one to seven days of treatment relapsed, but only 21 percent relapsed after twenty-two to thirty days of treatment. Time spent in treatment is directly related to success in recovery. Today, managed care administrators are often the ones to determine the length of treatment a patient requires—three to ten days of inpatient care is typical. Families are often faced with paying for additional inpatient care out of pocket.

Intensive outpatient treatment (IOP) typically meets four evenings a week for three-and-a-half hours. Once the assessment process is complete, patients don't receive individual counseling as a regular part of the program, but only on an as-needed basis. Some IOPs provide patients with medical exams upon admission to the program, but most don't. An IOP session begins with a short lecture followed by group therapy. Patients do not have access to the multiple services offered in inpatient treatment, as described above. There are very few IOPs designed for older adults.

Day treatment provides patients with more support than IOP, but less than residential care. In day treatment, patients attend a residential program during the daytime hours, but return home every afternoon. They participate in all the activities of the inpatient program except the evening activities. Day treatment is often used as a transition phase after inpatient treatment is completed. Patients attend three to five days a week, according to the level of support they need.

Outpatient treatment is a lower level of care than IOP. Typically, patients receive one ninety-minute group session per week. This level of care is augmented with frequent or daily attendance at Alcoholics Anonymous meetings. This is usually a step down after completing a more intensive treatment program.

A federal law on confidentiality protects people in treatment. Patients must sign a release form before staff can provide information to anyone outside the treatment center. Without a release, staff cannot confirm whether an individual is in the treatment program, nor can they talk to family members.

But relatives can provide staff with information. If your relative doesn't sign releases for family members, write down the pertinent facts about his or her addiction, the negative consequences it has caused, and any other relevant information. Send the letter to the clinical supervisor of the treatment center. He or she will share the information with the other members of the clinical team. Family information is an important part of assessing older adults' needs, because denial and memory loss prevent patients from reporting accurately on their chemical dependency.

In addition to treating the alcoholic, treatment centers offer family programs to educate and support relatives and friends. Studies show that when relatives attend family programs, alcoholics do better in treatment.

♒

Special Treatment Needs of Older Adults

Older adults do best in programs designed for people their age. Grouped with young people addicted to crack, marijuana, and heroin, older adults feel they don't belong. Needs are different between the young and the old, as are perceptions and lifestyles.

Older adults progress more slowly in all areas—detoxification, transition from one level of treatment to the next, walking from place to place, grasping new concepts, openly talking about feelings, and regaining mental sharpness. Older adults fatigue more quickly. They require shorter program sessions and longer rest periods. Hearing and vision limitations may restrict an older adult's ability to participate in treatment. Cognitive and physical problems impede reading and writing abilities. Older adults require a simple, slow treatment program that responds to these special needs.

Detoxification from alcohol or other drugs takes more time. The drugs used to withdraw older adults from alcohol or medications are shorter acting, so the older adult's thinking isn't adversely affected. But shorter-acting drugs require closer medical supervision and frequent monitoring of vital signs. Older adults sometimes *decompensate*—they get worse before they get better. They exhibit more health problems, have difficulty walking, and show greater cognitive impairment. With the support of a clinical team trained to monitor and treat decompensation, most older adults recover in a few days without hospitalization.

Maxine came into treatment functioning fairly well. She was stable physically and fairly alert. She went through the medical detox without major problems, but five days into treatment, her vital signs changed. Her blood pressure elevated, and she began experiencing anxiety. She had some difficulty walking, and her thinking dulled. She complained of pains she didn't have upon admission. Maxine's family was alarmed that she was worse after several days of treatment. The treatment staff assured the family that older adults sometimes appear to "fall apart" once the alcohol or other drugs begin leaving their systems, but in time and with proper support, they regain equilibrium.

Early in treatment, older adults are reluctant to talk about problems with alcohol or medications, but they will talk about their lives. Evelyn came into treatment afraid and ashamed. She'd raised three children and had five grandchildren, but now she felt branded by the label *alcoholic*. But when her counselor was interested in her life, not just her drinking, Evelyn's sense of self was restored. Evelyn talked about her broken heart over the death of her old dog, the charming and funny things her three-year-old granddaughter said, the accomplishments of her grown children, and her love of gardening. Each time Evelyn met with her counselor, she began by talking about her life—memories, disappointments, and hopes. Evelyn began likening her counselor to a good friend or a daughter, and she became comfortable with opening up about her alcoholism. By talking about her life first, Evelyn was finally able to talk honestly about how chemical dependency affected her life.

Preserving an older adult's dignity is a primary goal of age-specific treatment. Older adults value good manners and respectful communication. Counselors show respect by adopting the manners and deportment of the older adult. Counselors ask older adults how they prefer to be addressed, use language the older adult won't find offensive, and treat the older adult with affirmation rather than confrontation.

Treatment designed for younger people centers on group therapy, with individual counseling limited to a few sessions per week. Older adults need more frequent contact with counselors, sometimes daily meetings. Without one-to-one daily contact, older adults lose their sense of direction and become overwhelmed with problems. Counselors keep them on track by talking about their progress in treatment and helping them find solutions to problems.

Older adults do better in age-specific treatment programs, but few programs exist. If there are no older adult programs in your home area, the resource section of this book lists older adult programs in different parts of the country. If going out of state for treatment is not an option for your older relative, find a treatment center that treats a significant number of older adults—10 to 15 percent of its general population. Ask the clinical director of the program if he or she will individualize treatment to address the needs of your older relative. Will they keep the treatment plan simple, build in rest periods, more frequent one-to-one counseling sessions, and compensate for the older adult's slower pace? Are any staff members experienced in geriatrics? Is treatment nonconfrontational? What is the likelihood that your older relative will have an older roommate? Do they offer specialized therapy groups for older adults, such as grief groups? Is the medical team equipped to handle the older adult's health issues and impairments?

When investigating treatment centers, use the following questions as a guide to determine if a facility will serve the needs of your older parent or relative:

- *Is the medical detox regimen designed for the older patient?* Detox is often longer for older adults, and detox medications used for younger populations are often not appropriate because they cause increased confusion and cognitive difficulties.
- *Does the older adult participate with primarily other older patients during all or many of the treatment activities?* Older

adults have difficulty identifying with younger adults being treated for addiction to illegal drugs, and they are offended by some of the language used by this population.

- *Are the group therapy sessions designed for the older adult?* Older patients are less inclined to share freely in group therapy because they were raised "not to air your dirty laundry." For this reason, group facilitators must take a more active role in the group and use an approach appropriate for this age group.
- *Are counselors and other staff members trained to counsel older patients?* Older adults do not respond well to direct confrontation, and they take longer to build a rapport with counselors. It is important that counselors build trust by inviting conversations about the older adult's children, grandchildren, pets, and other important aspects of their lives.
- *Does the older adult have daily individual contact with his or her counselor?* Unlike younger patients who do most of their work in group sessions, older patients benefit from daily one-on-one contact with a counselor.
- *Is the treatment team multidisciplinary?* Ask about the staff. A treatment team can include doctors, nurses, a psychologist, addiction counselors, a recreation specialist, a nutritionist, a chaplain, and a relaxation specialist.
- *Does treatment planning reflect the fact that older adults progress more slowly in treatment?* Rather than developing the entire treatment plan after an initial assessment with an older adult, weekly assessments and treatment planning throughout the treatment stay may be required.
- *Does the schedule build more time between appointments?* Older patients often walk more slowly or need assistance to get from place to place, so scheduling should reflect this need.
- *Are regular rest periods built into the schedule?* Oftentimes, older patients will not admit they need a rest, even when

staff members ask. Scheduled rest periods for all ensure they get the rest they need.

- *Is treatment based on the Twelve Steps of Alcoholics Anonymous?* For quality, long-term sobriety, the Twelve Steps of Alcoholics Anonymous are central to a program of recovery. Does the treatment center use the Twelve Steps in their treatment, and do they offer Twelve Step meetings? Are older adult Alcoholics Anonymous meetings offered?

- *Are special services available if the older adult has trouble caring for him- or herself?* If an older adult has limited mobility or difficulty bathing, does the center engage the service of caregivers or aides, and is there an additional fee for these services?

- *Are older adults screened for limitations that can block recovery?* If the older adult has hearing loss, limited vision, or other problems, does the center offer materials designed for these special needs, such as large-print books and handouts, and books and pamphlets on tape? Even the color of paper used for handouts can affect how clearly the older adult can read the material.

- *Is a high level of family involvement encouraged by the treatment staff?* Family involvement is always important, but even more so with older patients. Does the staff update the family frequently (if a release of information is signed by the patient)? Does the center provide a family program? Is the family involved in aftercare planning?

- *Are specialized groups provided that address issues related to, but that extend beyond, chemical dependency?* Helpful groups include grief groups, leisure and recreation planning, life transition groups, sober living skills, relaxation techniques, and computer/Internet classes.

- *Does the center offer older adult aftercare?* Older adults do best in an aftercare group composed of their peers and offered during daytime hours. Some older adult aftercare groups offer lunch in the treatment center's cafeteria as a further incentive to attend. Aftercare can become a social outlet increasing the likelihood of regular attendance, which is important to successful recovery.

• *Are transportation services available for day treatment, aftercare groups, or other outpatient activities?*
• *What are the costs of the program? Are there additional costs for additional services?* Is funding available for low-income seniors? If a treatment center's fees are beyond what you can afford, ask them for referrals to funding agencies, low-cost treatment, and no-cost treatment.

⚑

A Tour of an Older Adult Treatment Program

This tour is based on standards set by the Hanley-Hazelden Center's inpatient program for older adult treatment. Older adult programs vary, but you can use this as a measuring stick for evaluating different programs. The tour gives you an idea of what your older relative will experience once he or she is admitted into treatment.

Admissions: Upon arrival, the older adult will meet with an admissions counselor. Family members are invited to participate in the admissions process. The counselor will complete paperwork, finalize financial details, and ask the older adult to sign release-of-information forms so the counseling staff can communicate with his family and his physicians. Once admitted, the older adult is transferred to the nursing unit. The family says good-bye to the older adult at this point.

Nursing Unit: The nursing staff interviews the older adult about his medical history. They collect the older adult's medications and ask for a complete list of all prescription and over-the-counter drugs he uses. The physician begins a detoxification regimen using medications that don't heavily sedate older adults. Nurses check vital signs more frequently to monitor withdrawal symptoms and administer medications as needed. The next day, the physician meets with the older adult to do a complete physical exam including bloodwork and drug testing. The doctor and nursing staff determine if the patient has limitations that will block treatment—hearing, vision, speech, incontinence, mobility, or cognitive impairment—and make recommendations to treat or offset them. Once the patient is medically stable, he is transferred to an older adult unit for chemical dependency treatment.

Older Adult Unit: Facilities for older adults can vary widely. Some are based in hospitals, and others are freestanding and have a homelike atmosphere. Our tour is through a freestanding facility designed with an island resort decor. The community room on the unit is well-appointed with rattan furniture, a dining area, a small kitchen stocked with snacks and beverages, and double glass doors leading to a patio with a water fountain and garden. Patients' rooms each accommodate two older adults, so they interact with one another rather than remain isolated from each other. Each room has a wall divide between beds for extra privacy, individual writing desks, and closets. Bathrooms have handicap access including walkout showers. The older adult unit is attached to the nursing unit, so patients have immediate access to medical services. A chapel provides older adults a quiet place to think, meditate, or pray.

The grounds of the treatment center are landscaped with flowers, shrubs, and trees. Walking trails circle a small lake. A gazebo is a favorite spot for conversations, and an outdoor pool provides exercise and relaxation time. A bookstore stocks personal necessities patients may need while in treatment. A hairdresser, manicurist, and masseuse are available by appointment. Many older women say yes to accepting help after learning they can get their hair and nails done while in treatment.

Once the older adult is on the unit, he is assigned a counselor who meets with him daily. The counselor works with the treatment team, and together they assess the older adult's needs. The psychologist assesses whether the patient has psychological problems or dementia by administrating tests and then consulting with the patient. If the older adult is diagnosed with a psychiatric disorder in addition to the chemical dependency, he is referred to the psychiatrist. Problems such as depression can be caused by chemical dependency and, if so, will clear up in recovery. But if the problem exists separately from addiction, it requires separate treatment. Two primary problems that exist separately but simultaneously are called a *dual diagnosis*. The psychologist will *co–case manage* the older patient with a dual diagnosis, working in tandem with the chemical dependency counselor to address issues that go beyond addiction. The older adult sees his counselor daily and the psychologist weekly. The psychiatrist prescribes nonaddictive medications as needed. (In hospital-based facilities, psychiatrists are often responsible for coordinating the chemical dependency treatment as well as prescribing medications for dual diagnosis.)

The older adult's counselor assesses the patient's chemical use history and determines if the diagnosis is chemical dependency. The patient and the counselor discuss how often the older adult used alcohol or other drugs, how much he consumed on the average, and what negative consequences he experienced due to the drug use. The counselor looks for symptoms that indicate chemical dependency: blackouts, passing out, protecting supply, hiding bottles or pills, preoccupation with using the drug, loss of control, increased or decreased tolerance, emotional isolation, social isolation, family problems, health problems, financial problems, loss of potential, ethical deterioration, endangering self or others. Not every alcoholic experiences all these symptoms, but as the disease progresses, the number of symptoms increases. Counselors also determine the pattern of drug use. For instance, a patient may have been a periodic drinker in his forties and fifties, but now drinks daily.

The counselor assesses the older adult's social history by talking about his family life, social relationships, education, career and retirement, financial condition, legal issues, and leisure-time activities. The counselor asks the older adult about his childhood, his relationships with his parents and his siblings, his marriage and children, and hobbies and recreation. This helps the treatment team determine which areas of the older adult's life need rebuilding or healing. If he has given up his hobbies and stopped seeing friends, the treatment team will help him reintroduce activities into his life and develop a leisure-time plan. If a brother or sister died when the older adult was a child, or a parent abused him, counselors help him work through his old emotional pains. If he no longer feels a purpose in life, counselors help him discover a new direction. If he hasn't grieved the death of a spouse, counselors help him begin the process.

The chaplain completes the spiritual assessment with the older adult. Spirituality is not religion. Spirituality is identified in two ways: positive spirituality and negative spirituality. A positive spirituality is defined as the willingness to reach out to others for help. A negative spirituality is the opposite—the older adult is emotionally shut down and unable to ask for or accept help. Recovery requires transforming a negative spirituality into a positive spirituality. The chaplain also determines if the older adult has strong religious beliefs or is agnostic or an atheist, and if these beliefs are strengths or blocks to recovery.

Family involvement during the assessment process is of paramount importance. Even older adults who are open and honest with their counselors are unable to accurately describe their addiction because delusional thinking has prevented them from seeing their problem clearly. Many adults, due to shame or denial, minimize the alcohol or other drug problems. They also rewrite family histories and leave out details, because they were raised not to discuss personal problems and to leave family "skeletons" in the closet. The counselor must talk with family members to get a complete picture of the older adult's needs. This must happen *before* the treatment plan is written. If the older adult has been in treatment for three days, and you have not been contacted by his counselor, initiate the call yourself. Counselors have very busy schedules, so give detailed information in the shortest time possible. Don't expect conversations with counselors to last for more than fifteen minutes. They have caseloads of six or more patients, and each patient has several family members. The counselor's free time between staff meetings, group therapy, individual sessions with patients, lectures, and paperwork is limited. So make a few notes before you call. Jot down how much alcohol or other drugs the older adult consumes and how often, problems he is experiencing due to his addiction, family problems, past problems he has not dealt with, and names of drinking buddies. The counselor will want to talk to two or three family members during the assessment process, but for ongoing progress reports, the counselor speaks to one family member who acts as the spokesperson for the family. As we discussed earlier, if the older adult has not signed a release of information, the counselor cannot contact the family, but the family can send an informative letter to the clinical director of the treatment program.

Once the family information is collected and the assessments are completed, the treatment team meets to develop a treatment plan based on the older adult's needs. The treatment plan is designed to teach the older adult how to work a program of recovery and restore a life damaged by addiction. The plan addresses physical, mental, emotional, and spiritual needs, because all of these areas are affected by addiction. Treatment plans set goals that, when achieved, surmount specific problems. Each goal is achieved by completing a series of assignments.

Assignments are designed to encourage the older adult to reach out to others for help. An assignment may require specific work in group therapy, talking about an issue with another patient, or individual discussions with counselors. The treatment team reviews the older adult's progress on his treatment plan on a weekly basis. If the older adult's work isn't satisfactory, the team determines what is blocking the older adult's progress and works with him to remedy the problem.

Throughout the assessment process and treatment, the older adult participates in a number of activities during the daytime and evening hours. Activities are educational and therapeutic. A typical day begins with all older adult patients participating in a motivational reading and meditation time before breakfast. Following breakfast, the recreation specialist leads the older patients in stretching exercises. Then patients attend a lecture followed by a discussion period. Next, the older adults go into group therapy, facilitated by one of the addictions counselors, for an hour. After group, they have lunch together in the cafeteria. After lunch, a rest period is scheduled. The remainder of the day is filled with a variety of specialized groups and activities: pool and recreation, nutrition education, grief group, Twelve Step groups, and discussion sessions. In late afternoon, patients have free time for working on assignments or meeting with counselors. After dinner, patients attend a lecture or meeting, or hear a speaker from Alcoholics Anonymous. Patients are in bed by ten o'clock.

Aftercare Planning: Before the older adult leaves treatment, the clinical team determines what level of support the older adult needs upon returning to his home. Recommendations are written up in an aftercare plan. The aftercare plan is the older adult's recovery program. It includes Twelve Step meetings, such as Alcoholics Anonymous, and support groups designed to help the older adult make the transition between treatment and home. Since older adults do not move quickly from one level of care to the next, aftercare plans often include step-down levels of treatment, such as day treatment or outpatient groups. The aftercare plan also addresses other issues, such as grief or health problems. Below is an example of an aftercare plan:

1. Upon discharge from treatment, attend day treatment three days a week for four weeks, following all of the treatment team's recommendations.
2. Attend the three-day family program to learn how your alcoholism has affected the people in your life and how your parent's alcoholism affected you as a child.
3. Attend the "Sober Seniors" Alcoholics Anonymous meeting each Wednesday at 12:00 P.M. Ask five older adult Alcoholics Anonymous members for their phone numbers, and call one person each day. Find an AA sponsor two weeks after leaving treatment.
4. Attend the older adult aftercare group on Wednesdays for a minimum of four months and discuss your strengths and challenges in recovery.
5. Continue grief counseling as counselor determines appropriate.
6. See your primary physician for ongoing medical problems.
7. Use relaxation techniques before going to sleep.
8. Implement a leisure-time plan by getting involved in sober activities during free time.

⚓

Groups Designed for Older Adults

Older patients experience age-related issues that cannot be ignored during treatment. Retirement, grief, health, empty-nest syndrome, loss of income, loss of youth—they must be part of the recovery process. If the pains of aging are ignored, they can contribute to a return to drinking or medication abuse. The following list describes some of the groups designed to treat both the problems of addiction and of aging, and to overcome older adults' reluctance to participate in the group therapy process:

Older Adult Group Therapy: Group therapy is the workhorse of treatment. Patients identify common problems and common solutions, and gain deeper insights into themselves and the complexity of their disease. But the decorum older adults bring to group therapy can sabotage the process. They are polite rather than honest. They don't confront fellow patients about denial, and they sidestep difficult issues. Civility gets in the way of helping each other gain a deeper understanding of their addiction. After Mary's first group therapy session, she left muttering, "I can't believe the counselor would be so rude as to suggest Frank wasn't telling the truth when he said he only had one drink a night!" Of course, the counselor knew from Frank's chemical use history that he drank a fifth of Scotch every day, mixing it with Xanax. Counselors must gently urge older patients to give honest feedback to one another.

Group therapy rules that apply to younger adults don't always apply to older adults. For instance, the rule that no one can leave the room once group has begun isn't realistic for seniors who have poor bladder control. Older adults frequently break the *no-cross-talk rule,* giving another patient advice rather than sharing insights based on similar experiences. An older adult with back pain may have to get out of his chair and walk around the room during group.

Women's Issues Group: Older women were often taught to

defer to men and please others. They may recede into the background rather than assert themselves, giving men the leadership roles. They've been trained to take care of others. When counselors ask them to focus on their own needs—a crucial step toward recovery—older women feel they are being selfish.

An all-women's group allows women to explore issues they wouldn't discuss with men, practice assertiveness skills, and build self-esteem. Older women talk about the stigma and shame endured by mothers and grandmothers who are alcoholic. They discuss the isolation they felt in their addiction, their "closet drinking," and the energy spent hiding their problems from the world. They also talk about body image, the body fat that comes with age, the reality of how they looked and acted when drinking, and the deterioration of their health due to addiction.

In a women's group, older women feel free to take on the leadership roles that build self-esteem. Women share humor and are at ease talking about their feelings with one another. They help each other with problem-solving and learning to take care of themselves before they take care of others.

Men's Issues Group: Older men have difficulty identifying feelings. They problem-solve and control, but they don't emote. Counselors direct them to rephrase their statements during group, using "I feel" instead of "I think." It's common to hear counselors ask men to "get out of their heads." Older men are comfortable intellectualizing and resist getting in touch with feelings and letting go of control—two important elements of recovery.

Older men don't have the body-image problems experienced by older women, but they grieve the loss of physical strength and the ability to do what they used to do. They rarely understand that their physical decline is more a consequence of drinking than age. Older men follow directions well and strive to be "winners." Both qualities are assets for recovery.

Grief Group: All older adults have grief issues. Sometimes grief is obvious—the death of a spouse or a child. Other times, grief is subtle—loss of youth or life roles. Even the loss of a relationship with alcohol is a grief issue. Some older adults grieve the loss of status in society after retirement. Others grieve the distance between themselves and their grandchildren. As long as older adults are drinking or abusing mood-altering drugs, they cannot work through their grief. For example, Joe lost his wife ten years ago. His alcoholism masked his grief and prevented him from coming to terms with his loss. In treatment, he was able to experience his feelings in a real way for the first time and begin the grieving process.

Life Transition Group: For many older adults, old age brings boredom, meaninglessness, loneliness, and powerlessness. Without a positive vision for the future, older adults become despondent and spiritually impoverished. Alcohol—used to fill up feelings of emptiness—deepens the void by robbing older adults of health, mental clarity, enthusiasm, and relationships.

Life transition group is a discovery process. It helps patients grow by finding a new purpose to life and making peace with life's losses. Older adults learn they have a choice: Treat age as an enemy or re-create life in spite of the limitations that come with age. As French writer Paul Claudel said: "Eighty years old: No eyes left, no ears, no teeth, no legs, no wind! And when all is said and done, how astonishingly well one does without them!"

Story Time Group: In the first week of treatment, older adults share the story of their chemical dependency with their peer group. They tell when the problem first began, what was going on in their life at that time, the repercussions they suffered, and what happened to get them into treatment. Story time is an icebreaker for older adults. By telling their story, they allow themselves to be vulnerable in front of their peer group. This is an act of trust and creates bonds between peers. By sharing their common experiences, older adults discover they are not alone in their disease, nor is it their fault. Story time is a powerful tool for breaking through denial and alleviating feelings of shame.

Lectures: Older adults attend two lectures a day. Lecture topics include alcohol's damaging effect on the human body, how mood-altering substances affect the brain, reaching out to others for help, relationships in recovery, working the Twelve Steps of Alcoholics Anonymous, spirituality, anger and resentment, building self-esteem, grief, shame, relapse prevention, and more. Education breaks down denial and equips patients with the tools for recovery.

Nutrition Group: Older patients often suffer from malnutrition, hypertension, weight problems, diabetes, and poor eating habits. The body's capacity for absorbing nutrients is limited by both old age and alcoholism. Proper nutrition rebuilds bodies ravaged by addiction and fosters mental alertness. Existing health problems can be improved and future problems prevented. Nutrition group stresses the importance of self-care in recovery.

Alumni Support Group: People who graduate from the older adult program return as alumni and talk with the older adults in treatment. They discuss the realities of living life sober and answer questions about attending Alcoholics Anonymous. They offer suggestions about rebuilding family relationships, what to say when people ask why they're not drinking, and how to cope with activities that include alcohol. For instance, Paul asks about attending his niece's wedding after leaving treatment. He's concerned about drinks served at the reception. An older adult alumnus may offer a few suggestions: attend the wedding and skip the reception, or go to the reception with a sober friend and leave early, if necessary; hold on to your drink so you don't mistakenly pick up someone's alcoholic drink; and attend an Alcoholics Anonymous meeting before or after the wedding. The real-life experiences of alumni have a powerful effect on older patients. They learn that while sobriety has great rewards, early recovery is not as easy as they think.

Older Adult Recreation: Exercise is an important part of recovery. Older bodies become weaker as a result of alcoholism and other drug addictions. A recreational specialist, working with the medical team, determines a safe exercise routine for each patient. Swimming, stretching, walking, and low-impact aerobics strengthen aging bodies and give the older adult a sense of empowerment. As the body grows stronger, the older adult begins to regain a sense of independence and develops a can-do attitude.

Leisure-time Planning: Chemically dependent older adults lose interest in social activities, hobbies, and friendships. Addiction is compared to a jealous lover—it demands full-time attention and pushes away people and other pastimes. Getting sober requires replacing the time spent drinking with enjoyable activities because an older adult who is lonely and bored will drink again. Older adults, equipped with a leisure-time plan when they leave treatment, return home ready to rejoin the world.

Although patient schedules differ from one facility to the next, treatment programs offer many similar groups and activities. The following schedule is adapted from the Hanley-Hazelden Older Adult Program. It gives you a picture of a typical day of treatment for older adults:

7:00	Morning Meditation Reading and Discussion
7:30	Breakfast
8:00	Stretching Exercises or Relaxation Therapy
8:30	Personal Time (work on treatment plan; meet with counselor)
9:15	Lecture
10:15	Older Adult Group Therapy
11:25	Rest Period
12:00	Lunch
12:30	Grief Group
1:30	Recreation/Leisure-time Planning (pool or gym)

3:00   Men's Issues or Women's Issues Group
4:00   Relapse Prevention Group
4:30   Free Time (work on treatment plan)
5:30   Dinner
6:15   Story Time Group
7:00   Alcoholics Anonymous Speaker and Discussion

Different groups are scheduled for different days of the week. For instance, nutrition group, life transition group, Twelve Step group, and "Sober Seniors" Alcoholics Anonymous are scheduled for another day. One afternoon a week is set aside for family visitation. Family programs are scheduled during weekends or evenings.

⚏

Issues in Early Recovery

Make Decisions Before Treatment Ends

Ask the tough questions, make the big decisions, and finalize crucial plans before the older adult leaves treatment. Use the treatment team to reevaluate the needs of the older adult now that he or she is sober. Counselors can help older adults and their families find workable solutions for a wide range of issues.

A good question to ask before the older adult is discharged from treatment is "What can we do to support the recovery process *and* honor our relative's right to make choices for herself?" A good format for answering this question is the *relapse agreement*. Not all treatment centers include *relapse agreements* as part of their discharge planning, so you may have to ask for one.

Start by setting up an appointment with the older adult and her counselor during the last week of treatment. During this meeting, ask your relative, "What do you want us to do if you return to drinking or using mood-altering medications?" Present this question directly to the older adult, not to the counselor. This gives the older adult a sense of control over her own recovery. If the older adult responds with an answer unbefitting to a good relapse agreement, the counselor will help her explore better choices. Ask the counselor to write the answers down in the form of a short statement giving family members directives for responding to a relapse, as agreed upon by the older adult.

Here's an example of a thirty-five-year-old daughter (Karen) and her sixty-four-year-old mother (Julia) meeting with the counselor to develop a relapse agreement:

> **DAUGHTER:** Mom, your counselor said that you'd like to go over your aftercare plan with me before we talk about our relapse agreement.
>
> **MOTHER:** Yes, Dear. These are the things the counselors believe I must do to stay sober when I return home. There are also some directions for taking care of a few other things, such as getting along since your father's death. I initially had a few objections about the

151

Alcoholics Anonymous meetings they recommend, but I've learned from the alumni who come to talk to us that this is what it takes to stay sober. So this is what I'll do. [Turning to the counselor] Do you want to read the aftercare plan to Karen?

COUNSELOR: Sure. Karen, if you have any questions as we go along, just let me know. [The counselor reads the aftercare plan. Karen has a few questions, which the counselor and her mother answer.]

DAUGHTER: I think the aftercare plan sounds very thorough, Mom. I'm glad you are in agreement with everything. Do you want to talk about our relapse agreement now? I feel confident you are going to do very well in recovery, but I think it's prudent that we plan ahead for possible setbacks. If nothing else, it'll give me peace of mind if I know what you want me to do if anything happens.

COUNSELOR: What specifically do you want to ask your mother, Karen?

DAUGHTER: Well, I want to ask her—

COUNSELOR: [interrupting Karen] Don't tell me what you want to ask her. Ask your mother directly.

DAUGHTER: [turning to her mother] Mom, I learned in the family program that one of the main reasons people relapse is that they stop following their aftercare plan. I worry that this could happen to you. What would you want me to do if I saw this happening?

MOTHER: I don't think we have to worry about that, Karen. I have no intention of not following my aftercare plan.

COUNSELOR: Julia, of course you intend to follow your aftercare plan. But your daughter is asking you what you would want her to do if that changes in the future. For instance, if you stop going to your meetings, would you want her to talk to you about that?

MOTHER: Well, I suppose that would be all right. Yes, I imagine if I stopped going to my meetings, I might be in for some trouble. [To her daughter] You can come to me and talk. But I don't want you breathing down my neck. If I don't go to a meeting for a couple days, that doesn't mean I've quit going.

DAUGHTER: Is it safe to say if you haven't gone to a meeting in two weeks that I can ask you if things are going all right? Should I ask to go to a meeting with you? I'd like to do that.

MOTHER: Yes, two weeks is a good amount of time. And, sure, you could come to a meeting with me. You might get an education about this AA stuff.

COUNSELOR: If Karen goes to a meeting with you, make sure it's an open meeting. You don't have to be a member of AA to attend open meetings. Also, many locations offer AA meetings and Al-Anon meetings at the same time, but in different rooms. You could go together, but attend your own meetings.

DAUGHTER: Can we take this a step further, Mom? I'd like to know what you'd want me to do if you started drinking or using tranquilizers again.

MOTHER: Yes, I suppose we should talk about that, too. But I really can't imagine it ever happening. I've really learned a few things since I've been here.

COUNSELOR: For the most part, no one plans to relapse. Your daughter's question is a good one. What would you want her to do?

MOTHER: Well, let me think. Would I have to come back here? After all, having had treatment once, I can't see going through it again. I'm not sure what my daughter should do. Maybe if she asked me to stop, I'd come to my senses.

COUNSELOR: My experience with relapse is that it isn't always easy to come to your senses. Would it be reasonable to say that if you drink again, you'll return here for an assessment? Then we could help you decide what kind of support you need to regain your sobriety. Shall we say your daughter will set up an appointment for you to return here for an assessment?

MOTHER: Yes. That sounds sensible. But don't count on seeing me! I don't plan on relapsing.

DAUGHTER: Are there questions you have for me, Mom? Or ways I can help you?

MOTHER: Your trust, Dear. That's what I need from you.

COUNSELOR: [to the daughter] You may have the urge to monitor your mother's every move, but you can't control her recovery. She is responsible for that. Let your mother work her program of recovery, and if she runs into trouble, you now know what she wants you to do. I'll write up the relapse agreement, and we'll all sign it. Then I'll make copies for each of us to keep. Julia, shall I also make a copy for each of your sons?

MOTHER: Yes, and my sister Anne.

DAUGHTER: Mom, what if I follow the relapse agreement, but you become angry with me and refuse to honor our agreement? What then?

MOTHER: That's a good point [chuckles]. The two of us have clashed in the past, and there's no reason to believe it couldn't happen again. [To the counselor] What would you suggest?

COUNSELOR: If your daughter comes to you with concerns, and the two of you cannot resolve them, bring in a professional counselor to help you work it out. You can talk with your aftercare counselor or call me.

If Julia relapses, she is likely to respond more favorably to a relapse agreement that she helped create. The agreement also sets up accountability for Julia—she knows her family will take action if she stops following her aftercare plan or starts drinking. Accountability is a powerful psychological force. Doctors and pilots in recovery, for instance, are very accountable to others. If they stop following aftercare plans or they relapse, they can lose their licenses and careers. For this reason, doctors and pilots have very high rates of success in recovery. Family accountability can have a similar impact on older adults.

Living arrangements and transportation are other important topics to discuss before older adults leave treatment. For instance, if an older adult isn't capable of living in her family home any longer, bring up this difficult topic while she still has the support of the counseling staff. Explore ways to honor the older adult's preferences, keep her as independent as possible, and ensure her safety and well-being.

Older adults who couldn't manage daily living tasks before treatment are frequently capable of taking care of themselves once they are sober. The counselors and medical team at the treatment center can help you determine your relative's competency level. Is she able to bathe, dress, eat, walk, and use the bathroom on her own? Can she handle tasks such as housecleaning, preparing meals, managing finances, taking medications, and accessing transportation? If she has problems in any of these areas, are they permanent or temporary?

Once needs are identified, work with the counselors and the older adult to determine how to meet those needs. Present the older adult with a variety of solutions and let her make the final decisions. The counselor will formulate decisions into the aftercare plan. For instance, the treatment team might include the following recommendations for an older adult who wants to remain in her home but needs additional help:

- Work with your son to evaluate your home using a home safety checklist and make all necessary changes.
- Hire a handyman whose services include heavy housework, repairs, yard work, snow removal, gutter cleaning, and other needed tasks.
- Use a housekeeping service once a week for light housework and laundry.
- Reevaluate your needs, asking your family for feedback, every six to twelve months and make adjustments as needed.

If the older adult is unable to drive and needs transportation services, arrange for these before she returns home. How will she get to Alcoholics Anonymous meetings? Her aftercare support group? Will the treatment center arrange for an Alcoholics Anonymous contact to pick her up and take her to meetings?

Research door-to-door shuttles, grocery stores and pharmacies that offer home delivery, and transportation services for older people. Some organizations, including senior centers, offer free or low-cost transportation.

If the older adult is no longer able to drive safely, but is unwilling to relinquish her driver's license, put yourself in her shoes for a minute. Giving up the right to drive is symbolic of lost freedom and the descent into dependence. Talk to her counselors and determine whether her driving problems were related to her chemical dependency. If so, will she be able to drive now that she is sober? If the answer isn't clear-cut, go to the resource section of this book to find the American Automobile Association's Web site for senior drivers. You can download a booklet called "How to Help an Older Driver" and a self-quiz called "Drivers 55+: Check Your Own Progress." You can also contact your state's motor vehicles bureau for guidance.

If you and the older adult live a distance apart from one another, talk about long-distance caregiving. The guide *Aging Parents and Common Sense,* published by The Equitable Foundation, recommends spending time at your aging parent's home so you know the challenges he faces and the resources available in his community. In addition, ask for the names of three people who care about your parent's well-being, such as a neighbor, friend, or clergyperson. With your parent's permission, talk with these people and give them your home and work numbers so they can contact you. Also, planning ahead and communicating frequently can help your parent remain self-sufficient. When older adults are capable of making decisions on their own behalf, and their health and safety aren't threatened, relatives should step back and let them discover what works for them, even if that means making some mistakes.

Old age is a time of letting go of many things. Keeping older adults as independent as possible preserves their sense of dignity and self-determination. As Bessie Delaney, age 101, said in the book *Having Our Say*, "When you get as old as we are, you have to struggle to hang onto your freedom, your independence."

⛧

Grief and Loss

In early recovery, unresolved grief can look like anger, panic, fear, depression, or loneliness. It can be somatized into chest pains, headaches, fatigue, illness, weight problems, appetite disturbances, sleep disorders, or stress. Rarely are these symptoms recognized as delayed reactions to grief. Left to fester, grief can lead the older adult back to alcohol or other drugs.

Grief is an emotional response to loss. For older adults, losses mount with the years. Children move out of the nest and raise grandchildren in other parts of the country. Bodies wrinkle and crease. Faces show the relentless march of time. Retirement erases identity. Family homes are sold. A spouse, child, or sibling dies. Friends die.

Addiction brings more loss. It erodes important parts of older adults' lives: interest in family and friends, ability to maintain responsible social behavior, capacity to stick to promises not to drink, health and mental acuity, relationships with spouses and children, and time spent with grandchildren. It takes away youthfulness, initiative, emotional control, peace of mind, cherished beliefs about God and life, and the will to live. It even takes away memories of the drinking experience. Ultimately, addiction robs older adults of dignity and the respect of others. These are grief issues, too.

Early recovery brings its own losses. Older adults lose their "reliable old friend"—alcohol. Saying good-bye to drinking or pills means farewell to easy relief from emotional pain, stress, boredom, and sleeplessness. Older adults presume that the loss of alcohol will adversely affect their social life. They worry what other people will think if they don't drink. Losing their "social lubricant," they fear they won't be as funny, witty, or charming. Their mental picture of themselves is tied to alcohol, and euphoric recall tells them that drinking was good. Alcoholics have positive assumptions about drinking or taking pills even when reality is quite different. They grieve giving up their old life for this new sober one.

An older adult's worldview can inhibit the grieving process. Older adults' reactions to grief are reflected in messages they heard growing up: Time heals all wounds. He's in a better place now. It's time to move on. Don't spread your sadness around. Don't speak ill about the dead. Why talk about the past? Keep busy and you won't feel the pain. Don't wear your heart on your sleeve. It's God's will. Don't look back. Life is for the living. Be strong.

Older men's experiences of grief are dictated by gender-specific messages: Be in control. Endure stress without giving in to it. Shoulder the pain. Men don't cry. Take it like a man. It's a sign of weakness to show emotion.

These messages deny grief. Older adults were taught to stuff feelings rather than process pain and adjust to loss.

You can help your older relative work through grief in a number of ways. The following examples are adapted from suggestions made by the American Association of Retired Persons (AARP):

- Talk about losses. Reminisce about a loved one who has died or show sincere interest about how life changes with age. Encourage the older adult to teach you about aging and coping with loss. Talking can help the older adult work through grief and help you contemplate your later years.
- Allow the older adult to live as independently as possible. Rather than taking over tasks, teach the older adult new skills that will help him run his own life.

- Encourage the older adult to make new friends, develop new interests, take up new hobbies, and learn new skills.
- Listen without trying to fix everything. Sometimes the older adult needs an attentive ear more than a problem-solver.
- Recognize that displaced anger may be a symptom of unresolved grief. Don't let the older adult's anger push you away, creating another loss in his life. Instead, help him find a vehicle for working through his emotions, such as attending a grief group.
- Write and visit frequently. Find fun things to do together. Ask grandchildren to come up with "random acts of kindness" for Grandma or Grandpa. Take the time to listen. Give hugs. Laugh. As people grow older, it is time with loved ones they value most.
- Don't hurry the older adult through the grieving process. As Shakespeare wrote, "Everyone can master a grief but he that has it." If the older adult stops talking about his loss after a few months, don't assume he's worked through it.
- Take one day every year to discuss the future. Talk about what events the next year will bring; make plans for family get-togethers and holidays; discuss health, finances, and living arrangements. Have an open discussion about goals, challenges, and blessings.
- Come up with new family traditions. Sometimes doing things the way they were always done accentuates loss. New traditions create new memories.
- Welcome changes and honor choices. Older adults make changes more easily when relatives accept the new lives they are shaping.

The above suggestions are supportive of recovery as well as the grieving process.

Older adults can process grief by participating in Alcoholics Anonymous. Getting a *home group*—which one member of

Alcoholics Anonymous described as "a place where everyone knows your name"—provides older adults with new friends. For example, Harry, a seventy-one-year-old recovering alcoholic, attends his home group every Saturday morning. After the meeting, all of the older men go out to breakfast together. "Retirement was the toughest thing I've ever done," explained Harry, "but these guys knew what I was talking about." The men created a safe network of friends from their home group and helped each other by sharing their experience, strength, and hope. Harry found that he needed the friendship of other men who understood his loss from a man's point of view. From this group of men, Harry found an Alcoholics Anonymous sponsor. The two of them meet twice a week for coffee. They've become good friends and often fish and golf together. The genuine friendships Harry made in Alcoholics Anonymous help him redirect energy away from his grief and into new relationships and activities.

There are several organizations that help people process grief. The American Association of Retired Persons offers the AARP Widowed Persons Services (WPS). A twenty-five-year-old, nationwide organization, WPS offers one-to-one outreach by trained widowed volunteers, group meetings, speakers, online discussion groups, publications, community referrals, and social activities. Most services are free of charge. Some support groups require a low fee to cover expenses. Social activities are "pay as you go." To locate an AARP Widowed Person Services program in the older adult's home area, call 800-424-3410 or e-mail griefandloss@aarp.org. To join the AARP Online Grief Support Discussion on America Online, enter the keyword "AARP." Then click the "Chat Rooms" icon. Next, click "Events," and then click "Enter Event Chat Room." Chats are held Monday, Tuesday, and Thursday nights.

Hospice offers excellent grief groups. Find a local group by contacting Hospice Foundation of America at 202-638-5419 or online at www.hospicefoundation.org. You can also call the

National Hospice Organization at 800-658-8899. Compassionate Friends offers services nationwide to parents who have lost a child of any age. They also offer support to grandparents and siblings. There are no membership fees or dues, and they can be contacted toll-free at 877-969-0010 or online at www.compassionatefriends.org. The National Family Caregivers Association offers a bereavement kit designed for former caregivers to help them through the first year of loss. The kit costs ten dollars for nonmembers and can be ordered by calling 800-896-3650 or online at www.nfacares.org.

To locate pastoral grief counseling, call your church or synagogue. The American Association of Pastoral Counselors keeps a national database of pastoral counselors who use spiritual resources as well as mental health experience to help facilitate healing and growth. To find a counselor, call 800-225-5603 or go online at www.aapc.org. When contacting the counselor, ask if he or she is trained and experienced in grief counseling.

Older adults need skills in processing grief as they prepare to face more losses in the years to come. Old age, it has been said, is an island surrounded by loss. As Judith Viorst explains in her book *Necessary Losses:*

> We lose not only through death, but also by leaving and being left, by changing and letting go and moving on. And our losses include not only our separations and departures from those we love, but our conscious and unconscious losses of romantic dreams, impossible expectations, illusions of freedom and power, illusions of safety—and the loss of our own younger self, the self that thought it always would be unwrinkled and invulnerable and immortal. . . . These losses are part of life—universal, unavoidable, inexorable. And these losses are necessary because we grow by losing and leaving and letting go.

Older adults who learn how to cope with losses are resilient. As great a challenge as it is, the pain of loss, rightly experienced, can strengthen spiritual beliefs, sow compassion in the human heart, and deepen relationships.

⚞

Living Life Sober

Recovery is not just quitting drinking; it's learning to enjoy life sober. Living without alcohol can be a daunting task for many older adults, especially if they've had a close relationship with alcohol throughout most of their lives. But even late onset alcoholics will experience a huge void without alcohol or other mood-altering drugs. Contentment in sobriety requires filling this void. As the Big Book of Alcoholics Anonymous reminds us, "God willing, we . . . may never have to deal with drinking, but we have to deal with sobriety every day."

People are living longer than ever before. Once in recovery, most older alcoholics have years or decades of living ahead of them. A Harris Poll found that almost half the people aged sixty to sixty-nine refer to themselves as middle-aged, and so do one-third of people in their seventies. Eighty-four percent said they hope to live to be ninety years old. A picnic planned for forty-five centenarians in Tallahassee, Florida, was rescheduled when sponsors learned that half of the one-hundred-year-old honorees couldn't attend because they had vacation plans. "What to Call People Who Used to be Old," the title of an editorial that ran in the *New York Times,* focuses on the redefinition of aging as life spans increase and the old no longer feel old. The editorial writer, Dudley Clendinen, describes those over sixty-five as "people who feel younger, healthier, and less isolated than their parents did at the same age twenty-five years ago."

The book *Successful Aging,* written by John W. Rowe, M.D., and Robert L. Kahn, Ph.D., and based on the MacArthur

Foundation's study on aging in America, challenges what we once believed about aging. The study finds the following:

- "To be old isn't to be sick." Older people are more likely to stay healthy than become broken-down and decrepit. In fact, 89 percent of people aged sixty-five to seventy-four report no disabilities at all.
- "Old dogs do learn new tricks." Older people are fully capable of learning. Their mental alertness increases with regular physical exercise, strong social support, and self-confidence in handling life's challenges.
- "Inheriting good genes doesn't get much credit for healthy aging." Only 30 percent of physical aging can be attributed to heredity. In old age, environment and lifestyle are more important than genes.
- "Older adults aren't a burden; they pull their own weight." One-third of older adults have paying jobs and another third volunteer. Others work to help family, friends, and neighbors.
- "It's never too late." Clean living at any age reduces damage caused by a lifetime of harmful behaviors, such as smoking, drinking, eating a high-fat diet, and not exercising.

In the book *Everything to Gain: Making the Most of the Rest of Your Life,* former president Jimmy Carter and former first lady Rosalynn Carter say:

We all have limitations, and have to live with them. . . . However, if we are able to make clear assessments of our remaining opportunities with some degree of objectivity, there is a lot we can do to enrich our lives . . . we can add vitality to our lives by actively experimenting with new interests, tasks, and hobbies. Over the years, we ourselves have tried photography, woodworking, gardening, gourmet cooking, fly-fishing, oil painting, bird watching, collecting old bottles and Indian artifacts, building houses, writing books, and a wide range of sports.

Life satisfaction in early recovery increases for older adults who reinvest the energy they spent drinking into building a support system in Alcoholics Anonymous, following an exercise program, interacting with friends, spending time with family, taking up hobbies, engaging in sober activities, and volunteering. Recovery is about finding contentment, giving and receiving help, building relationships, taking risks, and having fun.

Alcoholics Anonymous is a social outlet for older adults in recovery. Alcoholics learn how to live sober from other recovering alcoholics. Those who have found meaning, purpose, and fun in sobriety bring hope to older adults newly in recovery. Many cities and towns have Alcoholics Anonymous clubs— places where recovering people can socialize and go to meetings. Clubs sponsor barbecues, dances, holiday parties, and potluck dinners. People stop by any time of the day or evening for a cup of coffee and to talk, tell stories, and joke with other recovering people. A sixty-eight-year-old successful business owner newly in recovery said, "I've never met more fun-loving and nonjudgmental people anywhere else in my life."

Exercise programs for older adults are available at senior centers, retirement villages, community centers, and health clubs. The MacArthur Foundation study found that regular exercise can make a substantial difference in the health and well-being of older adults. Weight training helps even the oldest people. Benefits—such as doubled muscle strength, weight loss, increased energy, relief from depression, and improved balance—show up in as little as three months. Weight training also reduces risk of falls, coronary heart disease, high blood pressure, and colon cancer. Aerobic exercise—dancing, hiking, walking, jogging, and swimming—can double an older adult's endurance and improve heart and lung functioning.

Volunteer work keeps older people engaged in life and provides them with purpose. Many organizations—hospitals, schools, nursing homes, churches, treatment centers, literacy projects, hospices, youth clubs, mentoring programs, environmental groups, community outreach programs, homeless shelters, and state and national parks—welcome volunteers. Alcoholics Anonymous programs ask for volunteers to greet newcomers, make coffee, and organize printed materials.

Several organizations match older adults with volunteer opportunities:

- *Volunteer Match* is a nonprofit organization that uses the Internet to help individuals nationwide find volunteer opportunities. Visit their Web site at www.volunteermatch.org.
- *Experience Corps* mobilizes the time, talent, and experience of older adults in service to the community. The primary focus is on youth and schools. Visit their Web site at www.experiencecorps.org or call 415-430-0141.
- *Generations United/Foster Grandparents* advocates the mutual well-being of children, youth, and older adults. Visit their Web site at www.gu.org or call 202-638-1263.
- *Senior Pen Pals,* sponsored by Senior Partners in Education, is looking for older adults to volunteer to write letters to a school-aged child for one academic year. This offers learning and emotional benefits to children, and it is a good volunteer opportunity for older people who have difficulty leaving home. Call 800-759-4723.
- *The National Retiree Volunteer Coalition* transforms the skills and expertise of retirees into community leadership and service. Visit their Web site at www.nrvc.org or call 800-899-0089.
- *National Senior Service Corps* was authorized under the Domestic Volunteer Service Act of 1973 and offers a variety of programs. Volunteers typically work on teams of four or more seniors. Visit their Web site at www.cns.gov or call 202-606-5000.

Trying something new introduces challenge and excitement into the lives of older adults. Sometimes older adults internalize myths about aging: "I'm too old to learn anything new." According to Dr. Rowe and Dr. Kahn, in their book *Successful Aging:* "The persuasive belief among young and old that the elderly cannot sharpen or broaden their minds creates a disturbing cycle of mental inactivity and decay. Certainly, the less people are challenged, the less they can perform. But research shows that older people can, and do, learn new things—and they learn them well." Older adults can find new adventures for mind and body through a variety of venues:

- Many specialty retail stores offer instructional classes: kitchen shops offer cooking courses; outdoor sports centers offer kayaking and fly-fishing lessons; garden stores and home-improvement centers offer "do-it-yourself" classes; craft supply stores offer an assortment of creative workshops; and bookstores offer live music, poetry readings, and author talks.
- Community centers and colleges offer adult education classes on everything from foreign languages to car maintenance, computers, the Internet, yoga, furniture refinishing, financial planning, water aerobics, and more.
- Senior centers offer classes, exercise programs, lectures, computer classes, social activities, and day trips. Public libraries offer book clubs, brown bag lunch series, and lectures. Churches offer potluck dinners, singles clubs, and study groups.
- Older adults can go back to college to get the degree they've always wanted. A few years ago, a woman was in the news for getting a Ph.D. at age seventy-five.
- Elderhostel, listed in the resource section of this book, offers local, national, and international travel adventures for older people at very reasonable prices. Sober Vacations International offers travel packages for recovering people. For a brochure, call 800-762-3738 or go to www.sobervacations.com.

- Senior magazines are great for sparking the imagination and learning what activities other seniors are enjoying. *Modern Maturity*, published by AARP, and *New Choices*, published by Reader's Digest, are excellent publications. A weekly Internet magazine for older adults called *Grand Times* is available at www.grandtimes.com.

Older adults sometimes brush aside suggestions of doing something new because they think, at their age, they won't do it well. A bit of wisdom from the senior page of a local newspaper puts these fears into perspective: "Never be afraid to try something new. Remember, an amateur built the Ark; professionals built the Titanic."

Grandparenting is possibly one of the most important roles in older adults' lives. When so many life roles have faded with time, fostering the grandparent role gives older adults opportunities to share the gifts that come with age: stability, time to listen, wisdom and moral values, patience, storytelling, rituals, nurturing, a slower lifestyle, and a lifetime of experiences. Grandchildren can strengthen relationships with grandparents by visiting, making phone calls, sending e-mail, and planning outings. Even when grandparents live far away, grandchildren can connect:

- Start a photo album by sending the album and cover page first. Once a month and on special occasions, send an additional page for the album with photos, drawings, notes, and poems.
- Send audiotapes with grandkids singing songs or telling stories.
- Help children plant a tree dedicated to Grandma or Grandpa.
- Send postcards from vacation spots.
- Record a video tour of the grandkids' school or tape sports events, ballet classes, birthday parties, school plays, or music lessons. Kids can make a "meet my friends" video.

- Help the grandkids draw a map from home to Grandma and Grandpa's house.
- Grandkids can e-mail information about Web sites they think their grandparents would enjoy.
- Make a video of the grandkids serenading Grandma or Grandpa by lip-synching to a recording of the grandparent's favorite song.

Catherine's grandson mailed her a full-sized paper cutout of himself and a disposable camera. Reading the book *Flat Stanley,* he had the idea to ask his grandmother to take a photo of herself and his cutout-self at the different places she visited on her cruise vacation. When she returned, she sent back the camera filled with shots of the "two of them" all over Europe. Catherine's grandson made a scrapbook from all the photos and presented it as a class project. He vicariously experienced faraway places with his grandmother, and both grandson and grandmother developed a closer bond.

The Internet and e-mail can open new worlds for older adults. Grandparents using e-mail can connect with grandkids on a daily basis no matter how far apart they live.

Web sites for people over fifty are available on every possible topic: health, retirement living, travel, hobbies, life transitions, managing money, grandparenting, senior housing, government services and benefits, grief and loss, online computer classes, grandchildren, and more. The resource section of this book lists numerous Web sites for older adults.

For older adults who don't own computers, Web TV is an inexpensive alternative. Internet sites and e-mail messages are displayed on the screen of the older adult's television set, and the large print is an important feature for some older adults.

Online Alcoholics Anonymous meetings and recovery chat rooms are available day and night. Hazelden hosts an older adult chat room at www.hazelden.org/events. Online meetings and chats are a good way for older adults to get started if they're reluctant to attend Alcoholics Anonymous meetings in their community or if they're housebound.

Recovery is about living life to its fullest. In many ways, older adults who find their way into Alcoholics Anonymous are happier with their lives than other retirees. An excerpt from a story in the Big Book of Alcoholics Anonymous titled "Those Golden Years," written by a retiree after five years of sobriety, illustrates this high level of satisfaction with life in recovery:

> When I retired, I said I'd never be bored. AA has not let me down there. How full it has kept my retirement years—the five I've lived since the first two lost in traveling a rocky road to hell, before I made a U-turn.
>
> Not long ago, I was lunching with another retired publicist. He was close to tears in describing his boredom without an activity. He said, "How I envy you for whatever you've found." He did not know it was AA, and it was useless to tell him, for he doesn't have our disease.
>
> I tried to encourage a search for some new goal. But I couldn't help thinking, "You poor guy. I feel so sorry for you. You're not an alcoholic. You can never know the pure joy of recovering within the fellowship of Alcoholics Anonymous."

No person is too old to benefit from treatment and recovery, and no alcoholic is hopeless. With recovery, life is fully lived, and the golden years begin to shine.

⚏

SECTION SIX

Resources

Older Adult Treatment Centers

Older adults often need greater support in treatment due to a more complex detoxification from alcohol or prescription drugs, multiple medical problems that can block treatment, memory loss, reduced mobility including difficulty driving, and slower overall progress in recovery. For this reason, inpatient treatment is often a better choice than outpatient treatment for older adults. Each person, however, should be assessed individually to determine the level of support that best meets his or her needs.

Call your state Agency on Aging or your state's director of substance abuse services for information on older adult treatment services in your home area.

Inpatient Treatment Services

Elders Substance Abuse Service at Jewish Memorial Hospital, 59 Townsend Street, Boston, MA 02119; (800) 564-5868. Housed within a medical hospital specializing in geriatric health services, the program offers structured addiction treatment for older adults. Provides two group therapy sessions per day and evening Twelve Step meetings. Staff includes a medical doctor and psychiatrist. Coexisting medical problems are addressed by the hospital staff. Age range is typically fifty-five and over. Length of stay varies. Detox ranges from three to seven days or longer, and rehabilitation ranges from fourteen to twenty-one days. Aftercare is referred out to other agencies. Medicare is accepted. Treats people from Massachusetts and neighboring states. One-third of the patient population is homeless.

Hanley-Hazelden Center Older Adult Program, 5200 East Avenue, West Palm Beach, FL 33407; (800) 444-7008. Web site: www.hazelden.org. A treatment program for people fifty-five years old and older who are addicted to alcohol or other drugs. This freestanding program is designed with a well-appointed, homelike atmosphere equipped with special amenities to accommodate up to eighteen older adults. A nursing unit is housed within the older adult structure. Patients have access to a swimming pool, serenity garden and courtyard, walking trail, gazebo, water fountains, a small lake, and a chapel for prayer and meditation. Treatment staff consists of chemical dependency counselors, medical doctors and nurses, a psychologist, a nutritionist, a recreation specialist, and a chaplain. A hairdresser, manicurist, and masseuse are available. A weekly older adult aftercare program is provided once treatment is complete.

Older Adult Inpatient Program at Chelsea Community Hospital, 775 South Main Street, Chelsea, MI 48118; (800) 328-6261. Web site: www.cch.org. An eight- to sixteen-day residential inpatient treatment program for older adults addicted to alcohol or drugs. Based in a community hospital, the program has beds for eight patients. The physician is a geriatrician and a board-certified addictionist. He uses acupuncture in addition to medications for detoxification. Patients see the physician and a therapist daily. Staff also includes nurses, a nutritionist, clergy, and a recreation specialist. Physical and occupational therapies are provided as needed. Medicare is accepted.

Older Adult Substance Abuse Program at Wake Forest University Baptist Behavioral Health, 3637 Old Vineyard Road, Winston-Salem, NC 27104; (336) 794-3550. The program is designed to meet the medical, social, emotional, and intellectual needs of older adults. Located in the Piedmont Triad area of North Carolina, this eighteen-bed residential program is designed for adults aged fifty-five and older. The program is associated with Wake Forest University Baptist Medical Center, a tertiary care hospital and medical school, and this association allows the treatment program to serve patients with medical conditions in addition to addiction. The program is scheduled to open February/March 2002.

Senior Treatment at the Ernie Turner Center, 4330 Bragaw, Anchorage, AK 99508; toll-free in Alaska: (800) 478-4786; outside of Alaska: (907) 561-5537. Web site: www.ernieturner.com. The center has an older adult track within the adult residential treatment program, offering thirty to ninety days of treatment. It is designed for people aged sixty and older. A nurse practitioner visits the center once weekly; no other medical services are provided. Staff addresses grief issues and facilitates older adult group therapy and individual sessions. Older adults mix with younger adult patients for some groups and activities. The center also specializes in the treatment of older adult Native Alaskans. Costs are on a sliding fee schedule. Day treatment is also available.

Outpatient Treatment Services

Kit Clark Senior Services: Alcohol Services for Older Adults and Gambling Treatment for Older Adults, 1500 Dorchester Avenue, Dorchester, MA 02122; (617) 474-1116. Outpatient treatment for older adults addicted to alcohol, medications, other mood-altering drugs, and/or gambling. Offers a full continuum of care including assessment services, individualized treatment plans, support groups, individual therapy sessions, and education. Staff can make house calls to older adults unable or reluctant to come to the center for an assessment. Offers Alcoholics Anonymous meetings. Clients can access services at the senior center such as lunches, adult day care, the health clinic, and various activities such as painting classes, exercise sessions, and parties. Staff will help clients find transportation services. Medicaid, Medicare, and private insurance are accepted for treatment services. Licensed by the Department of Public Health, which also covers individuals with no insurance.

Older Adult Recovery Center, 955 West Eisenhower Circle, Suite 5, Ann Arbor, MI 48103; (734) 665-5070. Offers older adult day treatment and aftercare for chemically dependent older adults aged fifty-five and over. Housing for out-of-town clients is available. A typical day lasts five to six hours and includes educational sessions and group therapy. Clients see a physician monthly.

⚶

Twelve Step Organizations

Al-Anon/Alateen Family Group, (888) 4AL-ANON. Web site: www.al-anon.org. Helps families and friends of alcoholics recover from the effects of living with the problem drinking of a relative or friend. Alateen is a similar program for youth. Call for meetings in the U.S. and Canada.

Alcoholics Anonymous, (212) 870-3400. Web site: www. alcoholics-anonymous.org. A fellowship of men and women who have had a drinking problem. It is nonprofessional, self-supporting, nondenominational, multiracial, apolitical, and available most places.

Debtors Anonymous, (781) 453-2743. Web site: www. debtorsanonymous.org. The goal is to live without incurring any unsecured debt and to help other compulsive debtors achieve solvency.

Dual Recovery Anonymous, (888) 869-9230. Web site: www. dualrecovery.org. Members are chemically dependent and also affected by an emotional or mental illness.

Families Anonymous, (800) 736-9805. Web site: www. familiesanonymous.org. A program for family members and friends concerned about someone's current, suspected, or past drug, alcohol, or related behavioral problems. Call for meetings in the United States and Canada.

Gam-Anon, (718) 352-1671. Composed of men and women who are husbands, wives, relatives, or close friends of compulsive gamblers.

Gamblers Anonymous, (213) 386-8789. Web site: www. gamblersanonymous.org. A fellowship of men and women who share their experience, strength, and hope with each other so that they may solve their common problem of gambling and help others.

Nar-Anon Family Groups. For friends and relatives of people addicted to illegal drugs or narcotics, and the special problems that result from living with those addictions. Consult your phone book for a listing.

Narcotics Anonymous, (818) 773-9999. Web site: www.na.org. A program that reaches out to people addicted to illegal drugs or narcotics.

Overeaters Anonymous, (505) 891-2664. Web site: www. overeatersanonymous.org. A program for individuals recovering from compulsive overeating.

Internet Twelve Step Meetings

Online Twelve Step meetings are helpful when an older adult cannot get to a meeting in his or her community, or can augment the meetings he or she already attends.

AA Online, www.aaonline.net. Produces open "facsimile AA" real-time topic meetings for alcoholics using AOL. Hosts fifty online Alcoholics Anonymous meetings per week. Anyone with a desire to stop drinking who subscribes to AOL can attend.

About.com, www.alcoholism.about.com. Click on "Meetings." Scroll down and choose online Alcoholics Anonymous, Al-Anon, or other Twelve Step meetings. Offers real-time chat meetings; voice-type chat rooms; e-mail discussion groups; Internet relay chats; women's e-mail meetings; meeting-after-the-meeting chat rooms open twenty-four hours a day; Spanish-speaking meetings; and recovery bulletin boards.

Cyber Sober, www.cybersober.com. Online meetings include Alcoholics Anonymous, Al-Anon, Gamblers Anonymous, Narcotics Anonymous, and Tobacco Anonymous. Recovery chat rooms.

Deaf and Hard of Hearing AA Twelve Step Recovery Resources, www.dhh12s.com. Lists online AA meetings.

Friends of Bill W., www.delphi.com/friendsofbillw/. Daily online Alcoholics Anonymous meetings. All meetings are open. To attend, you must fill out a short registration form.

Online Intergroup of Alcoholics Anonymous, www.aa-intergroup.org. Offers Alcoholics Anonymous e-mail groups, real-time groups, and bulletin boards. International Alcoholics Anonymous online groups are listed.

Sober City Pioneers, www.sobercity.com. Alcoholics Anonymous meetings every night. Offers video chat and message boards.

Sober Voices, www.sobervoices.com. Live voice meetings; Mac compatible. Offers Alcoholics Anonymous men's rooms, women's rooms, international rooms, French-speaking meetings, Marijuana Anonymous, and Al-Anon rooms.

Staying Cyber, www.stayingcyber.org. A series of weekly Alcoholics Anonymous meetings. "Coffee Pot Page" offers general discussions, sharing, jokes, announcements. Newcomers are asked to read the guidelines before participating in any meetings.

Recovery Resources

Nonprofit Associations and Government Agencies

Christians in Recovery, Web site: www.christiansinrecovery.com. An organization dedicated to mutual sharing of strength and hope each day in recovery. Discussion of the Twelve Steps, the Bible, and experiences in recovery.

Council of Special Mutual Help Groups, Web site: www. crml.uab.edu/~jah/. A collection of leaders in recovery, from various professional groups, providing support and networking to professionals recovering from alcoholism or other drug addictions. Professional groups include nurses, anesthetists, pharmacists, doctors, ministers and pastors, nuns, academics, psychologists, social workers, and veterinarians.

Jewish Alcoholics, Chemically Dependent Persons, and Significant Others, 426 West 56th Street, New York, NY 10019; (212) 397-4197. Web site: www.jacsweb.org. A coordinated movement of addicted Jews, significant others, and concerned professionals working together to encourage and organize the Jewish community to deal with the problem of addiction. Retreats, meetings, and spirituality pages.

National Association for Children of Alcoholics, (888) 554-2627. Web site: www.health.org/nacoa. Advocates for all children and families affected by alcoholism and other drug dependencies.

National Council on Alcoholism and Drug Dependence, 20 Exchange Place, New York, NY 10005; (212) 269-7797. Web site: www.ncadd.org. Represents the interests of alcoholics, other addicted persons, and their families. Programs include prevention, intervention, and treatment. Offers a variety of publications.

National Institute on Alcohol Abuse and Alcoholism (NIAAA), 6000 Executive Boulevard, Willco Building, Bethesda, MD 20892. Web site: www.niaaa.nih.gov. Supports and conducts biomedical and behavioral research on the causes, consequences, treatment, and prevention of alcoholism and alcohol-related problems. Publishes the quarterly bulletin "Alcohol Alert," which disseminates research findings on alcohol abuse and alcoholism.

Office of National Drug Council Policy, Web site: www.whitehousedrugpolicy.gov. Provides news including congressional testimony, speeches, and commentary. Lists facts and statistics about illegal drugs. Publications can be downloaded from the Web site.

Online Recovery, Web site: www.onlinerecovery.org. Offers a wide range of resources: self-help, Twelve Step meetings, treatment, discussion forums, events, chat meetings, and more.

⚓

Resources on Aging

In recovery, older adults are faced with issues that have been affected by, and go beyond, chemical dependency. Rebuilding a life in sobriety requires addressing the whole person, including health and wellness, leisure and lifestyle, finances and housing. The following resources provide a wide range of information in these areas of daily living. This information is also helpful to the families and caregivers of the older adult.

Health and Wellness

Alzheimer's Association, (800) 272-3900. Web site: www.alz.org. Provides support for people with Alzheimer's disease, their families, and their caregivers. Local chapters offer help lines, support groups, and education. Provides information on "Safe Return," a program for the identification and safe return of persons who wander off and become lost due to this illness.

Alzheimer's Disease Education and Referral Center, (800) 438-4380. Web site: www.alzheimers.org. Offers information about the latest research on Alzheimer's disease, new treatments, and clinical trials. Publications can be printed off the Web site or ordered by phone.

American Diabetes Association, (800) 342-2383. Web site: www.diabetes.org. Provides education about exercise, meal planning, sex, complications, diabetes supplies, a bookstore, a virtual grocery store, and legislative information.

American Geriatrics Society, (212) 308-1414. Web site: www.americangeriatrics.org. They will provide a list of physicians certified in geriatrics through the U.S. mail or by e-mail.

American Heart Association, (800) 242-8721. Web site: www.americanheart.org. Online risk assessment and a thorough cross-reference guide on heart attacks and strokes.

The American Lung Association, (800) 586-4872. Web site: www.lungusa.org. Online smoking cessation program; call or e-mail the ALA to ask questions or go to the FAQ page on the Web site.

Arthritis Foundation, (800) 283-7800. Web site: www.arthritis.org. Information about medicines, alternative and complementary therapies, water exercise, and easy-to-use products. Informational specialists answer questions by e-mail.

Healthfinder, Web site: www.healthfinder.gov. A free gateway to reliable consumer health and human services information developed by the U.S. Department of Health and Human Services. Helps you find publications, Web sites, support groups, government agencies, and nonprofit organizations.

Lesbian and Gay Aging Issues Network, Web site: www.asaging.org/lgain.html. Works to raise awareness about the special challenges that lesbian, gay, bisexual, and transgendered (LGBT) elders face. Offers a Web directory of Internet resources dealing with LGBT aging. A monthly update called "Outword Online" provides brief articles.

The Lighthouse National Center for Vision and Aging, (800) 334-5497; TDD line (212) 808-5544. Web site: www.lighthouse.org. Helps locate low-vision clinics in your home area.

Love First, Web site: www.lovefirst.net. Provides information about family intervention with a section on intervening on older adults.

The Many Faces of Aging, Web site: www.aoa.gov/may2001/default.htm. Information specific to African American elders; Hispanic American elders; American Indian, Alaska Native, and Native Hawaiian elders; Asian American and Pacific Islander elders; lesbian, gay, bisexual, and transgendered elders. Also provides fact sheets on the diversity of caregivers and cultural competency.

Meals on Wheels Association of America, (703) 548-8024. Web site: www.mealsonwheelsassn.org. Provides information on delivery of Meals on Wheels.

MEDLINE Plus, Web site: www.nlm.nih.gov/medlineplus. Online guide to over nine thousand prescription and over-the-counter drugs; dictionaries of medical terms; locations and credentials of doctors, dentists, and hospitals. Various health topics.

The Merck Manual of Geriatrics, Web site: www.merck.com/health/. Access the Merck Manual Home Edition on the Web site. This is a great reference for researching diseases and conditions that commonly affect older adults. An interactive version uses photos, videos, audio pronunciations, and more.

National Association for Continence, (800) 252-3337. Web site: www.nafc.org. Offers facts on incontinence, how to get help, and a catalog of programs and publications.

National Association for Hispanic Elderly, (213) 487-1922 or (626) 564-1988. Web site: www.aoa.dhhs.gov/aoa/dir/127.html. Works to ensure that older Hispanic adults have equal access to social service programs for older adults. Provides English- and Spanish-language articles, brochures, and audio/video materials.

National Caucus and Center on Black Aged, (202) 637-8400. Web site: www.ncba-blackaged.org. National organization focused on improving life for older African Americans. NCBA has developed twelve housing projects for low-income elderly persons.

National Coalition for Cancer Survivorship, (877) 622-7937. Web site: www.cansearch.org. Produces "The Cancer Survival Toolbox," a self-learning audio program that helps people with cancer meet the challenge of their illness. Read or listen to it online, or order free audiotapes. Available in English, Spanish, or Chinese. Includes a specialized program for the elderly.

National Eye Care Program, (800) 222-3937. Offers extensive services including free eye exams for those who cannot afford an exam or are without access to eye care. Also treats cataracts, glaucoma, and macular degeneration through a network of ophthalmologists.

National Eye Institute, (301) 496-5248. Web site: www.nei.nih.gov. Provides fact sheets on age-related macular degeneration, cataracts, diabetic eye disease, and glaucoma. Sponsors a low-vision education program.

National Family Caregivers Association, (800) 896-3650. Web site: www.nfcacares.org. A grassroots organization created to educate and support people who care for the aged or chronically ill. Provides a quarterly newsletter for family caregivers, resource guides, news articles, reading lists, and other resources.

National Institute of Diabetes, Digestive and Kidney Diseases, Web site: www.niddk.nih.gov. Information on clinical trials, research, health topics, and education programs.

National Institute on Aging, (301) 496-1752. Web site: www.nih.gov/nia/. Works to understand the nature of aging and how to extend the healthy, active years of life.

National Osteoporosis Foundation, (202) 223-2226. Web site: www.nof.org. Talks about medications, finding a doctor, fall prevention, men and osteoporosis, support groups, and fashion tips for women with osteoporosis.

National Sleep Foundation, (202) 347-3471. Web site: www.sleepfoundation.org. Provides a toll-free telephone screening for daytime sleepiness: (877) BE-AWAKE. Publishes the magazine sleep*matters*. Offers education on insomnia, sleep apnea, and other sleep disorders.

National Stroke Association, (800) 787-6437. Web site: www.stroke.org. Provides survivor and caregiver resources, prevention programs, and topic-specific, in-depth articles and video webcasts.

The National Women's Health Information Center, (800) 994-9662. Web site: www.4women.gov. Information for women of all ages.

RnetHealth, Web site: www.rnethealth.com. Topics include stress and anxiety, chronic illness, drug abuse, depression, well-being, tobacco, alcohol, eating, and more. Offers live chats and information about their cable television network.

Self Help for Hard of Hearing People, (301) 657-2248. Web site: www.shhh.org. Works to enhance the quality of life for people who are hard of hearing. Publishes *Hearing Loss: The Journal of Self Help for Hard of Hearing People.*

Lifestyle and Leisure

AAA Foundation for Traffic Safety, (800) 305-7233. Web site: www.seniordrivers.org. Provides online self-quizzes to test your traffic safety acumen, including "Drivers 55-Plus Self Rating Quiz" and audio clips for the "Older and Wiser Driver." Order the free booklet "How to Help an Older Driver" or download and print the PDF version.

American Association of Retired Persons (AARP), (800) 424-3410. Web site: www.aarp.org. A compendium of useful and entertaining information for older adults including computers, health, leisure and fun, travel, spirituality, money, tax aid, research, volunteering, legislative issues, grandparenting, health care options, and legal services. Offers live webcasts, e-mail newsletters, magazines, online discussion center, webletter, and more.

Elderhostel, (877) 426-8056. Web site: www.elderhostel.org. Not-for-profit organization providing educational adventures for people aged fifty-five and over. Each program consists of one to four weeks of activities. Programs take place almost anywhere in the world and explore almost any subject. Shorter local programs take place in towns across the country. A free online catalog is available, or order a paper catalog. Average cost for a five-night program in the United States is under $500, which includes accommodations, all meals, classes, field trips, and accident insurance.

ElderWeb, Web site: www.elderWeb.com. Provides the online "Eldercare Locator" that searches out services, businesses, associations, and professionals by name, type, or location.

Frugal Living, Web site: www.frugalliving.about.com. Select "Frugal at Any Age" and then scroll down to "Senior Citizens." Subjects include cutting medication costs, discounts and good deals, ways to increase cash after retirement, and a bulletin board for penny-pinching ideas.

National Shared Housing Resource Center, (507) 433-8832. Web site: www.nationalsharedhousing.org. Provides two categories of services: match-up programs to help homeowners find a compatible home seeker who will pay rent or provide services in exchange for rent reduction; and shared-living residences where a group of people live cooperatively as an unrelated family in a large dwelling.

Older Women's League, (800) 825-3695. Web site: www. owl-national.org; e-mail: owlinfo@owl-national.org. A national grassroots organization focusing on issues unique to women as they age.

The Online Community for Seniors, Web site: www.senior.com. Offers current news stories, senior chats, cook's chats, e-mail clubs, computer classrooms, book clubs, Bible discussion, widow and widower support, and more.

Resources for Seniors, Web site: www.jobsearch.about.com/ careers/cs/resourcesforseni/. Job, career, and employment resources for older adults. Topics include freelance jobs, suggestions about age issues on resumes, staffing services for mature workers, articles on senior employment, job suggestions, internships for seniors, part-time and temporary jobs, and more.

Senior Living, Web site: www.seniorliving.about.com. Subjects include active living, computers, daily living, grandparenting, hobbies, nostalgia, pets, safety, and more.

Seniors-Site, Web site: www.seniors-site.com. Offers thirty information categories including classified ads for seniors, books for seniors, medical insurance, sleep disorders, widowhood, computers/Internet, and more.

Third Age, Web site: www.thirdage.com. Dedicated to first-wave baby boomers moving into older adulthood. Topics include beauty and style, computers, health, love, money, travel. Activities include chats, discussions, e-mail tools, free classes, games, and more.

Law and Government

Administration of Aging (AoA), 330 Independence Avenue SW, Washington, DC 20201; (202) 619-7501. Web site: www.aoa.gov. Offers a variety of directories: State Agencies on Aging; State Long Term Care Ombudsman; State Legal Assistance Developers; Area Agencies with Web Sites; and AoA Regional Offices. Provides information about "The Older Americans Act," older persons and their families, the national family caregiver program, and more. All information is available on the Web site.

Department of Veterans Affairs, (800) 827-1000. Web site: www. va.gov. Operates all veteran services. Web site offers easy access to information on health benefits and services, pension benefits, life insurance, and memorial benefits.

First Gov for Seniors, Web site: www.seniors.gov. A comprehensive Web site designed to help older adults find the government agencies appropriate for their needs. Provides links to the Web sites for state aging agencies and federal agencies. Other departments include consumer protection, legislation, retirement planner, seniors and computers, tax assistance, and more.

Housing and Urban Development (HUD), (888) 569-4287. Web site: www.HUD.gov/groups/seniors.cfm. Runs low-income housing for seniors. Use the Web site to research subjects such as staying in your home, finding an apartment, "housing plus help," protecting yourself, and staying active. Lists toll-free numbers for HUD-approved housing counselors.

Medicare Hotline, (800) 633-4227. Web site: www.medicare.gov. The hot line assists with questions about plans and HMOs, handles complaints, accepts reports of fraud, and takes orders for brochures. On the Web site, search health plans, nursing homes, dialysis facilities, Medigap policies, participating physicians, and more. Spanish and Chinese versions are available.

National Senior Citizens Law Center, 1101 14th Street NW, Suite 400, Washington, DC 20005; (202) 289-6976; and 3435 Wilshire Boulevard, Suite 2860, Los Angeles, CA 90010-1938; (213) 639-0930. Web site: www.nsclc.org. Advocates nationwide to protect the independence and well-being of low-income elderly individuals. Areas of law include age discrimination, Social Security, guardianships, health insurance, home health care, Medicare, pension rights, and more.

Senior Law, Web site: www.seniorlaw.com. A Web site to help seniors, their families, and attorneys and other professionals access information about elder law. Subjects include Medicare, Medicaid, estate planning, trusts, and the rights of the elderly and the disabled. Provides a list of lawyers specializing in elder law.

Social Security Administration (SSA), (800) 772-1213. Web site: www.ssa.gov. Runs Social Security retirement, disability insurance, Supplemental Security Income (SSI), and survivor's benefits. Find a directory of local offices on the Web site plus get answers to most of your questions about SSA.

⚓

Books and Publications

Carter, Jimmy. *The Virtues of Aging.* New York: Ballantine Publishing Group, 1998. The former president discusses the blessings that come with aging, and the special gifts older adults have to offer others.

Colleran, Carol, and Joseph Moriarity. *Problems with Alcohol and Medications among Older Adults.* Center City, Minn.: Hazelden, 1996. A multimedia series including a video, workbooks, and facilitator's guides. To order, call (800) 328-9000.

De Castillo, Maria Esther B. *Libre de Addiciones.* Mexico: Promexa, 2001. Spanish. Addresses addiction recovery, including codependency, from a culturally sensitive prospective. It incorporates Hispanic culture and religious/spiritual beliefs.

DuPont, Robert L., M.D. *The Selfish Brain: Learning from Addiction.* Center City, Minn.: Hazelden, 2000. Explores the biological roots of addiction and the ways addicts are allowed to deny their addiction by compassionate, well-meaning people.

Gomberg, Edith Lisansky, Ph.D. *Sober Days, Golden Years: Alcoholism and the Older Person.* Minneapolis: Johnson Institute, 1982. Booklet, 44 pages. To order call (800) 328-9000 and ask for item #3263.

Griffith, H. Winter, M.D. *Complete Guide to Prescription and Nonprescription Drugs.* New York: Perigee Books, 2000. Complete descriptions of medications, prescribed and over-the-counter. Includes how to take and store drugs, the effect of alcohol or other substances when mixed with a medication, how a drug can affect alertness, dosage and overdose, possible side effects, information specific to people over age sixty, and more.

Jay, Jeff, and Debra Jay. *Love First: A New Approach to Intervention for Alcoholism and Drug Addiction.* Center City, Minn.:

Hazelden, 2000. Teaches families how to motivate an addicted loved one to accept treatment using a *love first* approach. Clear, concise, and easy to use.

Ketcham, Katherine, and William F. Asbury. *Beyond the Influence: Understanding and Defeating Alcoholism.* New York: Bantam Doubleday Dell, 2000. Clearly explains the neurochemical nature of the disease of alcoholism, and explains what needs to be done to treat alcoholism.

Kominars, Sheppard, and Kathryn Kominars. *Accepting Ourselves and Others: A Journey into Recovery from Addictive and Compulsive Behaviors for Gays, Lesbians, and Bisexuals.* Center City, Minn.: Hazelden, 1996. Second Edition. Addresses the relationship between substance abuse and being a sexual minority.

Lesieur, Henry R., Ph.D. *Understanding Compulsive Gambling.* Center City, Minn.: Hazelden, 1986. Pamphlet, 32 pages. An overview of addictive gambling and its effect on lives, finances, and families. To order call (800) 328-9000 and ask for item #5497.

McGee, Gloria, et al. *Black, Beautiful, and Recovering.* Center City, Minn.: Hazelden, 1985. Pamphlet, 20 pages. For African Americans in the early stages of recovery from substance abuse. Takes into consideration cultural perspectives. To order call (800) 328-9000 and ask for item #1219.

Metlife Juggling Act Study: Balancing Caregiving with Work and the Costs Involved. Westport, Conn.: Metlife Mature Market Institute, 1999. Findings from a national study by the National Alliance of Caregivers and the National Center on Women and Aging. For a free copy call (203) 221-6580 or e-mail MMI_MetLife@metlife.com.

Samples, Pat. *Daily Comforts for Caregivers.* Minneapolis: Fairview Press, 1999. Offers gentle guidance and support for those overwhelmed by the day-to-day struggles of caregiving.

Samples, Pat. *Older Adults after Treatment: A Right to Recovery.* Center City, Minn.: Hazelden, 1989. Pamphlet, 25 pages. Discusses aftercare issues for older adults completing treatment. Topics include family relations, health, medications, and relapse. Offers tools to maintain recovery. To order call (800) 328-9000 and ask for item #5134.

Samples, Pat. *Older Adults in Treatment: Understanding and Healing.* Center City, Minn.: Hazelden, 1989. Pamphlet, 24 pages. Examines our beliefs about addiction in older adults and helps define chemical dependency as a disease. To order call (800) 328-9000 and ask for item #5137.

Wegscheider Cruse, Sharon. *Another Chance: Hope and Health for the Alcoholic Family.* Palo Alto, Calif.: Science and Behavior Books, 1989. Describes how the entire family is affected by one person's alcoholism and the roles family members subconsciously adopt to cope with the problem.

Wilkinson, James A. *A Family Caregiver's Guide to Planning and Decision Making for the Elderly.* Minneapolis: Fairview Press, 1999. Offers forms, checklists, and practical advice on health, housing, finances, and more. The author is an attorney specializing in health law.

⚏

Videos

The Doctor Is In: Substance Abuse in the Elderly. Lebanon, N.H.: Media Services of Dartmouth-Hitchcock Medical Center. Profiles older Americans dealing with problems related to alcohol and mood-altering prescription drugs. To order call (877) 884-6872.

It Can Happen to Anyone: Problems with Alcohol and Medications among Older Adults. Center City, Minn.: Hazelden and

AARP. Educational and awareness-building video. To order call (800) 328-9000 and ask for item #5736.

Schneider, Max A., M.D. *Looking Forward to Tomorrow: Medical Aspects of Seniors and Substances.* Carpinteria, Calif.: FMS Productions, Inc. An awareness video for anyone providing services for older adults, including doctors, medical schools, senior centers, elder care facilities, and hospitals. To order call (714) 771-8080 or (800) 421-4609.

⚖

Self-quizzes

The following quizzes are designed to help you determine if an older family member has a problem with alcohol or other drugs and how you've been affected. These quizzes are not scientific diagnostic tools. Weigh the results of each quiz in the context of your situation and use common sense.

Quizzes should not be used as a way to confront an addicted older family member with his or her problem. It would be destructive, not helpful, to present one of these quizzes as proof of addiction to the person you are concerned about. Rather, use the quizzes as one tool in the process of deciding how to best help your loved one and yourself.

Quiz: Signs of Alcoholism and Drug Abuse in Older People

The signs of alcoholism and drug addiction can be different in adults fifty-five years old and over than they are in younger people. The following signs of an alcohol or other drug problem are typical of the older adult:

☐ Prefers attending events where drinking is accepted, such as luncheons, happy hours, and parties.

☐ Drinks in solitary, hidden from others.

☐ Drinks more than before.

☐ Drinks the same or less yet still experiences problems.

☐ Makes a ritual of having drinks before, with, or after dinner. Becomes annoyed when this ritual is disturbed.

☐ Has lost interest in activities and hobbies that used to bring pleasure.

☐ Drinks in spite of warning labels on prescription drugs.

☐ Has bottles of tranquilizers on hand and takes them at the slightest sign of disturbance.

☐ Is often intoxicated or slightly tipsy, and sometimes has slurred speech.

☐ Secretly disposes of large volumes of empty beer and liquor bottles.

☐ Suffers from tremors and shakes.

☐ Makes excuses to keep liquor in the house (for guests, special occasions, and so on).

☐ Drinks despite health problems.

☐ Frequently expresses a wish to die.

☐ Often has the smell of liquor on his or her breath or uses mouthwash to disguise it.

☐ Neglects personal appearance and gains or loses weight.

☐ Complains of constant sleeplessness, loss of appetite, or chronic health problems that seem to have no physical cause.

☐ Has unexplained burns or bruises and tries to hide them.

☐ Seems more hostile or resentful than usual.

☐ Neglects home, bills, pets.

☐ Can't handle routine chores and paperwork without making mistakes.

☐ Has irrational or undefined fears and delusions, or seems under unusual stress.

☐ Seems to be losing his or her memory.

☐ Falls asleep during conversations.

☐ Appears to be depressed.

☐ Calls at odd hours.

☐ Has problems with urinary incontinence.

☐ Suffers from heart arrhythmia.

☐ Is involved in activities during evening hours.

Many of the symptoms listed above are attributed to other diseases or are considered part of the aging process. However, many older people find that once they achieve sobriety, these symptoms disappear.

Adapted from the pamphlet How to Talk to an Older Person Who Has a Problem with Alcohol or Medications, *published by Hazelden and available at no cost by calling (800) I-DO-CARE or (800) 436-2273.*

⚓

Quiz: Are You Troubled by Someone's Drinking?

The following questionnaire was designed by Al-Anon to help you decide whether Al-Anon is right for you. As you take this quiz, keep in mind that you may have been affected by a parent's drinking when you were a child.

1. Do you worry about how much someone else is drinking?
2. Do you have money problems because of someone else's drinking?
3. Do you tell lies to cover up for someone else's drinking?
4. Do you feel that if the drinker loved you, he or she would stop drinking to please you?
5. Do you blame the drinker's behavior on his or her companions?
6. Are plans frequently upset or canceled or meals delayed because of the drinker?
7. Do you make threats, such as, "If you don't stop drinking, I'll leave you"?
8. Do you secretly try to smell the drinker's breath?
9. Are you afraid to upset someone for fear it will set off a drinking bout?
10. Have you been hurt or embarrassed by the drinker's behavior?
11. Are holidays and gatherings spoiled because of drinking?
12. Have you considered calling the police for help in fear of abuse?
13. Do you search for hidden alcohol?
14. Do you often ride in a car with a driver who has been drinking?
15. Have you refused social invitations out of fear or anxiety?
16. Do you sometimes feel like a failure when you think of the lengths you have gone to in order to control the drinker?
17. Do you think that if the drinker stopped drinking, your other problems would be solved?

18. Do you ever threaten to hurt yourself to scare the drinker?
19. Do you feel angry, confused or depressed most of the time?
20. Do you feel there is no one who understands your problems?

Copyright © 1980 Al-Anon Family Group Headquarters, Inc.

Are Prescription and Over-the-Counter Drugs Used Safely?

To reduce the risk of an older adult's medicine misuse, use this quiz to determine whether drugs are being used safely.

☐ Are all doctors informed of all drugs used (including over-the-counter drugs, vitamins, herbal remedies, and alcohol)?

☐ Are doctors given a complete list of drugs now being used before a new drug is prescribed?

☐ Are directions for drug use—including possible side effects, what to do if a dose is forgotten, possible interactions with other drugs—clearly understood by the older adult?

☐ Does the older adult keep, in his or her wallet or purse, an updated list of all drugs used including name, dose, and frequency?

☐ Is the older adult mixing pills into the wrong bottles?

☐ Can the older adult differentiate the colors of different pills? Older adults lose the ability to see certain colors, so don't use directions such as "Take the blue pill twice a day, and the yellow once."

☐ Does the older adult take medications prescribed for someone else?

☐ Is a drug reference guide put to use to learn everything about every drug taken?

☐ Does the older adult keep medications that change mood or cause drowsiness someplace other than the bedside table (to avoid accidental overdose)?

☐ Does the older adult put on his or her glasses and use good light to read prescription bottles every time medications are taken?

☐ Are the labels on nonprescription medications read thoroughly?

☐ Is a standardized measuring spoon from the pharmacy used for liquid medications?

☐ Are diet instructions followed when using medications that require special dietary needs?

☐ Are medications stored properly—away from the heat and humidity in places such as bathrooms—and thrown out when expired?

☐ Does the older adult check with the doctor before changing a dosage or discontinuing use?

☐ Is one pharmacist used for all prescription and over-the-counter medications?

☐ Does the older adult need a Medic-Alert identification bracelet, and does he or she wear it?

☐ Does the older adult abstain from driving when using medications that cause drowsiness?

☐ Is the doctor promptly notified of any symptoms that may be caused by medications?

☐ Prior to surgery, is the doctor or dentist informed of all drugs taken in the last month or cortisone drugs used in the past two years?

☐ Is the doctor informed of the amount of alcohol used by the older adult?

☐ Is the older adult using medications intended for short-term use over a prolonged period of time (months or years), such as sleeping pills?

⚊

Index

About the Authors

DEBRA JAY is in private practice as an interventionist specializing in chemically dependent older adults. She provides intervention training and consultation services to families throughout the United States and Canada. Coauthor of *Love First: A New Approach to Intervention for Alcoholism and Drug Addiction,* she writes a regular newspaper column on alcohol and drugs in society. Ms. Jay resides in Grosse Pointe, Michigan, with her husband and two dachshunds. She can be reached at the Web site address www.lovefirst.net.

CAROL COLLERAN is the director of the Center of Recovery for Older Adults at the Hanley-Hazelden Center at St. Mary's in West Palm Beach, Florida. The lead consultant to Wake Forest University Baptist Behavioral Health for the development of an older adult alcohol and drug treatment program, Ms. Colleran is a participant in policy development and studies for several national organizations, including the Substance Abuse and Mental Health Services Administration, the National Council on the Aging, the Center of Alcohol and Substance Abuse at Columbia University, and the Millennium Assembly Task Force, a part of the United Nations Millennium General Assembly. Author of two books and numerous articles, Ms. Colleran has also produced videos in cooperation with AARP, participated in an award-winning PBS video series, and appeared on *The Today Show, Good Morning America,* and the *NBC Nightly News with Tom Brokaw.*